Surviving Narcissistic Abuse

From Confusion and Turmoil to Clarity and Strength

K.C. Lockwood

CHAPIESKI PUBLISHING

© Copyright K.C. LOCKWOOD [2024] - **All rights reserved.**

The content within this book may not be reproduced, duplicated or transmitted without direct written permission from the author or the publisher.

Under no circumstances will any blame or legal responsibility be held against the publisher, or author, for any damages, reparation, or monetary loss due to the information contained within this book. Either directly or indirectly. You are responsible for your own choices, actions, and results.

Legal Notice:

This book is copyright protected. This book is only for personal use. You cannot amend, distribute, sell, use, quote or paraphrase any part, of the content within this book, without the consent of the author or publisher.

Disclaimer Notice:

Please note the information contained within this document is for educational and entertainment purposes only. All effort has been expended to present accurate, up-to-date, and reliable, complete information. No warranties of any kind are declared or implied. Readers acknowledge that the author is not engaging in the rendering of legal, financial, medical or professional advice. The content within this book has been derived from various sources. Please consult a licensed professional before attempting any techniques outlined in this book.

By reading this document, the reader agrees that under no circumstances is the author responsible for any losses, direct or indirect, which are incurred as a result of the use of the information contained within this document, including, but not limited to, — errors, omissions, or inaccuracies.

Contents

Introduction	1
Chapter 1: Understanding Narcissistic Abuse	5
Chapter 2: The Impact on the Victim Chapter	15
Chapter 3: Practical Strategies for Immediate Relief	27
Chapter 4: Rebuilding Self-Esteem	39
Chapter 5: Setting and Maintaining Boundaries	51
Chapter 6: Navigating Relationships Post-Abuse	63
Make a Difference with Your Review	75
Chapter 7: Legal and Safety Considerations	77
Chapter 8: The Role of Therapy and Professional Help	89
Chapter 9: Mindfulness and Holistic Healing	99
Chapter 10: Parenting and Protecting Children	111
Chapter 11: Personal Empowerment and Growth	123
Chapter 12: Long-Term Recovery and Maintenance	133
Conclusion	143

| Keeping the Healing Alive | 147 |
| References | 149 |

Introduction

It's a chilling fact that nearly one in three people will experience some form of narcissistic abuse in their lifetime. This insidious form of manipulation can leave lasting scars, affecting not just the individual but entire families.

Narcissistic abuse is more common than we might think. It lurks in the shadows of many relationships, eroding self-worth and causing deep emotional turmoil. This abuse cuts across all demographics, affecting men and women alike. The impact is profound, leading to anxiety, depression, and even PTSD. The numbers are staggering, but the personal stories behind those statistics are even more heartbreaking.

I understand this all too well as I, myself, am a survivor of narcissistic abuse. I know the confusion, the doubt, and the pain that comes with it. I have walked this path myself, not just as a victim but also as a parent trying to shield my children from its toxic reach. My experiences have equipped me to help others navigate their own journeys towards healing and empowerment.

This book is for you—the men and women who have experienced the torment of narcissistic abuse. It's also for those who want to support loved ones going through it. You will find actionable steps and exercises designed to guide you through understanding, coping, and eventually overcoming the trauma inflicted by narcissistic abuse.

So, what is narcissistic abuse? In simple terms, it's a pattern of behaviour where one person uses manipulation, control, and emotional exploitation to dominate another. This can take many forms, including gaslighting, love bombing, hoovering, and employing flying monkeys to do their bidding. These tactics are designed to confuse you, make you doubt your reality, and keep you under their control.

Recognizing these behaviours is the first step towards breaking free. Gaslighting makes you question your memory and perception. Love bombing overwhelms you with attention and affection, only to pull it away later. "Hoovering" sucks you back in just when you think you're free. "Flying monkeys"—third parties who do the narcissist's bidding—add another layer of manipulation. Understanding these tactics will help you see through the fog and reclaim your life.

The purpose of this book is straightforward. I want to provide you with practical tools, exercises, and assignments that will help you understand, navigate, and heal from narcissistic abuse. Whether you're dealing with a narcissistic partner, co-parenting with one, or trying to rebuild your self-esteem, this book will be your guide.

Let's take a look at what you can expect from each chapter. We'll start by diving deep into understanding narcissistic behaviours and their impact on you. Then, we'll move on to strategies for co-parenting with a narcissist, focusing on setting boundaries and protecting your children. Finally, we'll explore ways to achieve emotional empowerment, offering steps to reclaim your self-worth and establish emotional independence.

What will you gain from this book? First and foremost, you will find validation for your experiences. You are not alone, and your feelings are real and valid. You will also gain practical recovery steps, strategies for self-care, and tools for rebuilding your life. This book aims to be a lifeline, offering support and guidance as you navigate this challenging journey.

Co-parenting with a narcissist presents its own set of challenges. Narcissists often use children as pawns, creating a toxic environment that can harm their emotional well-being. Setting boundaries is crucial, as is finding ways to protect your children from the narcissist's manipulative tactics. This book will offer specific strategies to help you navigate these tricky waters.

Healing is a journey, not a destination. The main steps for healing that we will explore include recognizing the abuse, reclaiming your self-worth, and establishing emotional independence. These steps are not easy, but they are possible. With time, effort, and the right tools, you will rebuild your life and emerge stronger than ever.

I encourage you to actively engage with the content of this book. Complete the exercises, reflect on the assignments, and trust the process. Healing and empowerment are within your reach, and this book supports you every step of the way.

As we embark on this journey together, I want you to know that there is hope. You have the strength within you to overcome this. You can heal, grow, and find peace. This book is your companion, offering guidance, support, and a roadmap toward a brighter future. Let's take this journey towards healing and empowerment with confidence, knowing that you are not alone and have the power to reclaim your life.

Chapter 1: Understanding Narcissistic Abuse

You're sitting at a family gathering, and someone brings up their latest achievement. Before they can finish their story, another person jumps in, making the conversation all about them. They boast about their success, dismissing the original speaker's accomplishment. This scenario might seem familiar, and it's a small glimpse into the world of narcissistic behaviour. But for many, interactions with narcissists go far beyond annoying conversation hijacks—they can become a source of profound emotional abuse and trauma.

Narcissistic abuse is a topic that needs more awareness and understanding. It's not just about dealing with someone who has an inflated ego; it's about recognizing and addressing the manipulation, control, and emotional exploitation that come with it. This abuse can leave lasting scars, affecting both the individual and their loved ones.

As a survivor of narcissistic abuse, I've seen firsthand the devastating impact it can have. I aim to help you navigate this difficult terrain, providing the tools and insights you need to reclaim your life and sense of self-worth. This chapter seeks to lay the groundwork by helping you recognize the traits and behaviours of narcissists so you can start to see through the fog and take the first steps toward healing.

1.1 Recognizing Narcissistic Traits

Narcissistic Personality Disorder (NPD) is a clinical diagnosis "characterized by a pervasive pattern of grandiosity, a need for admiration, and a lack of empathy" Stranieri, G., De Stefano, L., & Greco, A. G. (2021). PATHOLOGICAL NARCISSISM. According to the DSM-5, NPD falls under Cluster B personality disorders, which also include Antisocial, Borderline, and Histrionic Personality Disorders. Individuals with NPD often exhibit an inflated sense of self-importance, believing they are superior to others and deserving of special treatment. This grandiosity is not just a slight exaggeration of their abilities; it's an ingrained aspect of their personality that drives much of their behaviour. They frequently fantasize about unlimited success, power, brilliance, or beauty and expect to be recognized as superior even without achievements that warrant it.

Another core characteristic of NPD is a profound lack of empathy. Due to their lack of empathy, narcissists often have difficulty understanding or valuing the feelings and needs of others, which allows them to manipulate and exploit people without feeling guilt or remorse. They view others as extensions of themselves, tools to be used for their own gratification. This is why they often engage in manipulative behaviours, such as lying, gaslighting, and emotional blackmail, to maintain control over their victims.

Narcissists also have an insatiable need for admiration. They thrive on attention and praise, constantly seeking validation from others to bolster their fragile self-esteem. This need for admiration often leads them to monopolize conversations, belittle others, and exaggerate their achievements. They are preoccupied with fantasies of success, power, and brilliance and usually believe they can only be understood by, or should only associate with, other high-status individuals.

Common narcissistic traits include manipulative behaviours, an inflated sense of self-importance, exploitative relationships, entitlement, and arrogance. Manipulative behaviours are a hallmark of narcissism. Narcissists use various tactics to control and dominate others, such as gaslighting, triangulation, love bombing, hoovering, and flying monkeys.

- *Gaslighting* is a psychological form of manipulation where the abuser denies the victim's memories of an event, causing them to question their perception of reality and accusing the victim of "going crazy." The term "gaslighting" was coined from the 1938 British play called Gas Light, in which a husband manipulates a wife into thinking she is crazy by slyly changing the intensity of the gas lights in their home when she is left alone. He does this to make her believe she cannot trust herself or her memory.

- *Triangulation* is when a narcissist manipulates relationships by bringing a third party into the dynamic to create some form of conflict. This third party can be anyone – a friend, family member, ex-partner, colleague, or even an imaginary figure.

- *Love bombing* is when someone showers you with excessive or overwhelming levels of attention, affection and admiration. "The aim of this is to make the recipient feel dependent on and obligated to the individual," explains Alexander Burgemeester, a clinical psychologist and author from Amsterdam, the Netherlands.

- *"Hoovering"* is a manipulative tactic used to lure or suck a person back into a relationship they're withdrawing or stepping away from. It's a way of reasserting power and control and perpetuating a cycle of abuse. The word's origin is from the name of a vacuum cleaner manufacturer.

- *"Flying Monkeys"* refers to the people who carry out the work of a narcissist. It comes from The Wizard of Oz, referring to the monkeys who do the witch's bidding.

They have an inflated sense of self-importance, often exaggerating their talents and achievements while dismissing the contributions of others. In relationships, they are exploitative, using people to meet their own needs without regard for the other person's well-being. They believe they are entitled to special treatment and expect others to cater to their demands. Their arrogance is often displayed through haughty behaviours and attitudes, looking down on those they perceive as inferior.

Narcissism can manifest in different forms, including overt, covert, and malignant narcissism.

- *Overt narcissists* are the most recognizable. They are outgoing, arrogant, and entitled, often displaying their grandiosity openly. They crave attention and admiration and are not afraid to boast about their achievements.

- *Covert narcissists*, on the other hand, are more subtle. They may appear shy or humble, but underneath, they harbour the same grandiose fantasies and need for admiration. They often play the victim or use passive-aggressive tactics to manipulate others.

- *Malignant narcissists* represent the most dangerous form of narcissism. They not only display the typical traits of grandiosity and lack of empathy but also exhibit sadistic tendencies and paranoia. They derive pleasure from hurting others and are often vindictive and aggressive.

It's essential to differentiate between narcissism and healthy self-esteem. While narcissists exhibit arrogance, entitlement, and a lack of empathy, individuals with healthy self-esteem possess confidence, self-respect, and compassion. Healthy self-esteem is grounded in a realistic assessment of one's abilities and achievements. It leads to constructive behaviours and positive relationships. In contrast, narcissism is characterized by an inflated self-image and destructive behaviours that harm relationships. Narcissists often misinterpret constructive criticism as personal attacks and react defensively. However, those with healthy self-esteem can accept feedback and use it for personal growth.

Recognizing red flags in relationships is crucial for identifying narcissistic behaviour early on. One of the most common signs is overly charming and attentive behaviour at the beginning of a relationship. Narcissists often engage in love bombing, overwhelming their targets with affection and attention to create a sense of dependency. However, this initial charm quickly fades, and a pattern of quick attachment followed by sudden withdrawal emerges. Narcissists are also known for consistent blame-shifting and lack of accountability. They never take responsibility for their actions and always find a way to blame others for their mistakes or shortcomings.

Interactive Element: Red Flag Checklist

Take a moment to reflect on your past or current relationships. Use the checklist below to identify any red flags that may indicate narcissistic behaviour:

- Overly charming and attentive behaviour early in the relationship
- Quick attachment followed by sudden withdrawal
- Consistent blame-shifting and lack of accountability
- Monopolizing conversations and belittling others
- Expecting special treatment and favours without reciprocating
- Displaying arrogance and haughty attitudes
- Using manipulative tactics like gaslighting and triangulation

If you checked several of these red flags, you may have encountered a narcissist. Understanding these traits and behaviours is the first step toward recognizing and addressing narcissistic abuse.

In summary, recognizing narcissistic traits involves:

- Understanding the core characteristics of NPD.
- Identifying common narcissistic behaviours.
- Differentiating between types of narcissism.

- Distinguishing between narcissism and healthy self-esteem.

By learning to recognize these traits and red flags, you can protect yourself from falling into the trap of narcissistic abuse and begin the process of healing and reclaiming your life.

1.2 The Cycle of Narcissistic Abuse

The cycle of narcissistic abuse is a repetitive pattern that can trap victims in a continuous loop of emotional turmoil. Understanding this cycle is crucial for recognizing the dynamics of such relationships and taking steps toward breaking free. Typically, the cycle progresses through three main phases: *idealization*, *devaluation*, and *discard*. Each stage serves a specific purpose in the narcissist's quest for control and dominance, leaving the victim increasingly disoriented and vulnerable.

The **idealization phase** is where it all begins. The narcissist is charming, attentive, and seemingly perfect during this stage. They sweep their victims off their feet with over-the-top compliments and excessive praise. This stage can feel like a whirlwind romance, making the victim feel special and cherished. Narcissists are masters of mirroring, a tactic that mimics the victim's interests, values, and behaviours to create a sense of having a deep connection. This intense admiration and love-bombing are calculated moves to ensnare the victim, making them dependent on the narcissist's approval and affection.

Imagine meeting someone who seems to understand you completely, shares your passions, and showers you with compliments. It feels like you've met your soulmate. That's the power of the idealization phase. However, this stage is not genuine. It's a façade designed to hook you in and create a dependency on the narcissist's approval. The narcissist's goal is to build you up so they can later tear you down.

Once the narcissist feels they have secured their hold on the victim, the **devaluation phase begins**. This is where the mask starts to slip, revealing the true nature of the narcissist. Criticism and belittlement replace the once-flowing compliments. These put-downs can be subtle or overt, but their purpose is clear: to undermine the victim's self-worth. The gradual erosion of self-esteem is a hallmark of this phase. Narcissists use gaslighting to further destabilize them. They might say things like, "You're too sensitive" or "That never happened," causing the victim to question their perceptions and memories.

Triangulation is another tactic used during the devaluation phase. This tactic serves to make the victim feel insecure and desperate for the narcissist's approval. It's a calculated move to keep the victim off-balance and more controllable.

In the **discard phase**, the narcissist abruptly ends the relationship in a cold, often cruel manner. This can involve sudden withdrawal, where the narcissist cuts off communication without explanation, leaving the victim confused and hurt. They might also engage in smear campaigns, spreading false information to damage the victim's reputation and isolate them further. This phase is excruciating, as it often comes without warning, leaving the victim to grapple with feelings of betrayal and abandonment.

The psychological impact of each stage is profound. During the devaluation phase, the constant criticism and manipulation erode the victim's self-esteem. They begin to believe the negative things the narcissist says about them, leading to a deep sense of worthlessness. By the time the discard phase hits, the victim is left reeling with confusion and betrayal.

The sudden end of the relationship can trigger anxiety, depression, and even PTSD. The long-term effects of narcissistic abuse can include chronic stress, low self-esteem, and difficulties in forming healthy relationships.

Of all the aspects of narcissistic abuse, the role of intermittent reinforcement is one of the most insidious. This psychological concept explains how unpredictable cycles of affection and abuse keep victims hooked. The narcissist alternates between kindness and cruelty, creating a cycle of hope and despair. For example, after a period of intense criticism, the narcissist might suddenly become affectionate and loving again. This inconsistency makes the victim cling to the hope that the "good" version of the narcissist will return for good.

Intermittent reinforcement is powerful because it taps into the victim's deep-seated need for validation and approval. Becoming addicted to the highs and lows, the victim constantly seeks the narcissist's approval and fears their disapproval. It's a psychological trap that keeps them ensnared in the relationship despite the abuse.

The cyclical nature of narcissistic abuse means that this pattern often repeats, trapping the victim in a continuous loop. Even after the discard phase, the narcissist might re-engage the victim through a tactic known as "hoovering." Named after the vacuum cleaner brand, hoovering involves the narcissist attempting to suck the victim back into the relationship. They might use charm, apologies, or promises of change to lure the victim back. Unfortunately, these promises are rarely kept, and the cycle of abuse begins anew.

Victims of narcissistic abuse often find themselves hoping for change, yearning for the return of the idealization phase. They cling to the memory of the early days when the narcissist was charming and attentive. This hope is what keeps many victims trapped in the cycle despite the ongoing abuse. Recognizing this pattern is crucial for breaking free and beginning the healing process.

Narcissistic abuse can have long-lasting effects, but the first step toward breaking free is understanding the cycle. Each stage—idealization, devaluation, and discard—serves a purpose in the narcissist's quest for control. By recognizing these stages and the tactics used, victims can start to see the pattern and take steps to reclaim their lives. It's a difficult process, but with awareness and support, it is possible to break the cycle and find healing.

In recognizing the cycle of narcissistic abuse, you gain insight into the manipulative tactics used to control and dominate. This awareness is empowering, as it allows you to see through the narcissist's façade and understand the true nature of their behaviour. You are not alone in this experience, and understanding the cycle is crucial to reclaiming your life and rebuilding your sense of self-worth.

By identifying the stages of the cycle and the tactics used at each stage, you can begin to dismantle the psychological hold the narcissist has over you. The healing journey is not easy, and it starts with awareness and understanding. As we continue, we will explore practical steps and strategies to help you navigate and break free from the cycle of narcissistic abuse. Remember, you have the strength within you to overcome this and rebuild a life of clarity and strength.

Chapter 2: The Impact on the Victim Chapter

Imagine waking up every day feeling like you're walking on eggshells, constantly bracing yourself for the next emotional blow. This is the reality for many who suffer from narcissistic abuse. The daily grind of manipulation and control takes a profound and far-reaching toll. It's not just about the moments of overt cruelty but the insidious, relentless erosion of your emotional and physical well-being. Understanding the impact of this abuse is essential for taking the first steps toward recovery.

2.1 Emotional Exhaustion and Its Consequences

Emotional exhaustion is a state of feeling emotionally worn out and drained due to accumulated stress from your personal or work life. It's one of the most debilitating consequences of narcissistic abuse. Imagine being on a never-ending emotional roller-coaster. One moment, you're being showered with affection and praise; the next, you're subjected to harsh criticism and manipulation. This constant fluctuation leaves you in a state of perpetual anxiety, unable to relax or feel safe. Your mind becomes a battlefield, and your body bears the brunt of this unrelenting stress.

The cycle of emotional exhaustion stems from this continual emotional turmoil. The highs and lows create a sense of instability, making it impossible to find peace. You may find yourself constantly on edge, waiting for the next bout of criticism or manipulation. This chronic stress leads to a host of physical and mental health issues. Insomnia becomes a nightly struggle as your mind races with thoughts of past interactions and future anxieties. Sleep disturbances further exacerbate your exhaustion, leaving you feeling foggy and disoriented during the day.

As your emotional reserves deplete, your body begins to show signs of wear and tear. Increased susceptibility to illnesses becomes apparent as your immune system weakens under the constant strain. You might catch colds more frequently or experience other physical ailments that you never had before. Symptoms of depression and anxiety become your constant companions, further eroding your ability to function. The emotional weight becomes so heavy that simple tasks feel insurmountable.

This emotional exhaustion extends into your daily life, affecting your ability to perform everyday activities. Concentrating at work becomes a Herculean task, as your mind is preoccupied with the emotional chaos. You might find yourself making mistakes, missing deadlines, or lacking motivation to engage with your tasks. This can lead to further stress as you struggle to maintain your professional responsibilities.

Socially, you begin to withdraw. The energy needed to maintain relationships feels overwhelming, and you may find yourself isolated from friends and family. This withdrawal only deepens your sense of loneliness and despair. Neglecting personal care and responsibilities becomes another consequence of this exhaustion. Things that once brought you joy, like hobbies or self-care routines, fall by the wayside as you struggle to keep your head above water.

Given these profound impacts, finding ways to manage and mitigate emotional exhaustion is crucial. Prioritizing self-care becomes a lifeline. Start by setting small, achievable goals. This could be as simple as committing to a daily walk or setting aside time each day to engage in a hobby you enjoy. These small steps can create a sense of accomplishment and help rebuild your emotional reserves.

Mindfulness exercises are another powerful tool. Meditation, deep breathing, and yoga can help you reconnect with your body and mind, providing a sense of calm amidst the chaos. Mindfulness helps you stay present, reducing the overwhelming anxiety about the future or the lingering pain of the past. It's about finding moments of peace and clarity in your day, no matter how small they may be.

Interactive Element: Self-Care Checklist

Creating a self-care checklist can be a helpful way to prioritize your well-being. Consider including the following activities in your daily routine:

- *Physical Activity*: Aim for at least 30 minutes of exercise, whether it's a walk, yoga, or a workout.

- *Nutrition*: Plan and prepare balanced meals, focusing on nutrient-rich foods.

- *Sleep Hygiene*: Establish a bedtime routine to improve sleep quality.

- *Mindfulness*: Incorporate meditation, deep breathing, or journaling into your day.

- *Social Connection*: Reach out to a friend or family member for a chat or meet-up.

- *Personal Enjoyment*: Engage in a hobby or activity that brings you joy.

Incorporating these activities into your routine can restore your emotional and physical well-being. Remember, self-care is not a luxury; it's a necessity.

In conclusion, emotional exhaustion from narcissistic abuse is a significant and multifaceted issue. It affects every aspect of your life, from your physical health to your ability to function daily. By understanding the cycle of emotional manipulation and its consequences, you can begin to take steps towards recovery. Prioritizing self-care, setting achievable goals, and utilizing mindfulness exercises are practical strategies to help manage and mitigate the effects of emotional exhaustion. You have the power to reclaim your life and rebuild your strength, one step at a time.

2.2 The Erosion of Self-Worth

Narcissistic abuse chips away at your self-worth in insidious ways. It often begins with constant criticism and belittling. The narcissist zeroes in on your insecurities, magnifying them until they become almost insurmountable in your mind. You might hear phrases like, "You're too sensitive," or, "You can't do anything right." Over time, these words start to stick, planting seeds of doubt that grow into a full-blown lack of self-esteem. You start to believe that maybe you are overly sensitive, or perhaps you really can't do anything right.

In addition to direct criticism, narcissists frequently compare you to others in an effort to diminish your self-value. Statements like, "Why can't you be more like so-and-so?" or, "Look at how successful they are; what's your excuse?" are designed to make you feel inadequate. This manipulation is subtle but powerful, creating a constant sense of inferiority. You begin to measure yourself against unrealistic standards, always coming up short in your own eyes. This comparison game is a tactic to keep you feeling lesser, ensuring that you remain dependent on the narcissist for validation.

Narcissists also undermine your achievements and successes. When you accomplish something significant, rather than celebrating with you, they might dismiss it or downplay its importance. "That's not such a big deal," they might say, or "Anyone could have done that." By minimizing your accomplishments, they strip away your sense of pride and achievement, leaving you feeling like nothing you do is ever good enough. This constant undermining erodes your confidence, making you question your abilities and worth.

The long-term effects of this abuse are profound. Over time, you begin to internalize the negative beliefs imposed by the narcissist. These internalized beliefs become part of your self-identity, shaping how you see yourself and your worth. You might start to lose confidence in your personal abilities, doubting your capacity to succeed in various aspects of life. This self-doubt can lead to a reluctance to pursue goals and ambitions as you begin to believe that failure is inevitable. The dreams and aspirations you once had now seem distant and unattainable, overshadowed by the constant voice of criticism in your mind.

Consider the story of a professional who excelled in their career only to have their success constantly belittled by a narcissistic partner. Despite numerous promotions and accolades, they began to doubt their competence, feeling as though they had somehow fooled everyone around them. Another individual might question their attractiveness and desirability due to their partner's constant comparisons to others. These real-life examples highlight how pervasive and damaging narcissistic abuse can be, affecting every facet of a person's self-worth and identity.

Rebuilding self-worth after such profound erosion requires intentional effort and practical steps. One effective strategy is the use of affirmation exercises and positive self-talk. Start by identifying negative beliefs you hold about yourself and counter them with positive affirmations. For instance, if you find yourself thinking, "I'm not good enough," replace it with, "I am capable and deserving of success." Repeating these affirmations daily can help rewire your thought patterns, gradually shifting your self-perception.

Another crucial step is to identify and reconnect with your core values. These are the principles and beliefs that define who you are and what you stand for, which may have been overshadowed by the narcissistic relationship. Begin by engaging in value assessment exercises or worksheets that help pinpoint what truly matters to you. Reflect on past experiences when you felt most authentic and aligned with your values. These reflections serve as a guide to rediscovering and reaffirming your core values.

Aligning your actions with your core values can significantly enhance your self-esteem and confidence. Make decisions based on these values and strive to live authentically according to them. For example, if one of your core values is integrity, ensure that your actions reflect honesty and transparency in all your dealings. Living in alignment with your values boosts self-worth and provides a clear sense of direction and purpose.

Incorporating core values into daily life requires practical exercises and consistent effort. Keeping a values-based journal can be a helpful tool. Each day, jot down actions you took that aligned with your core values and reflect on how they made you feel. Setting goals that are aligned with these values can also provide motivation and a sense of accomplishment. For instance, if personal growth is a core value, set a goal to read a book or take a course that expands your knowledge and skills.

Understanding and recognizing your inherent strengths is another vital component of rebuilding self-worth. Conduct a strengths inventory by taking stock of your personal achievements and skills. Reflect on moments when you felt competent and proud of your abilities. Seeking feedback from trusted friends or family members can also provide valuable insights into your strengths. Often, others can see qualities in us that we might overlook or undervalue.

Reconnecting with passions and interests that bring you joy and fulfillment is equally important. Create a joy list by writing down activities that make you happy and fulfilled. These could be hobbies you once loved but abandoned due to the narcissistic relationship. Schedule time for these activities in your daily routine, and make them a priority. Engaging in activities that foster self-competence can reignite your sense of purpose and achievement. Whether it's painting, hiking, or playing a musical instrument, these activities can provide a much-needed boost to your self-esteem.

Additionally, seeking supportive and validating relationships is crucial in rebuilding self-worth. Surround yourself with people who uplift and encourage you rather than those who bring you down. These relationships can provide a safe space for you to express yourself and receive the validation you need. Building a support network of friends, family, or support groups can offer the encouragement and affirmation that is essential for healing and growth.

2.3 Cognitive Dissonance in Abusive Relationships

Cognitive dissonance is a psychological concept that describes the discomfort experienced when holding two contradictory beliefs simultaneously. In the context of an abusive relationship, this dissonance is particularly potent. You might find yourself wrestling with the reality of your partner's abusive behaviour while still clinging to the belief that they can be loving and kind. This internal conflict creates an emotional storm that is hard to navigate. One moment, you recognize the harm being done to you; the next, you're rationalizing their behaviour, convincing yourself that they didn't mean it or that you somehow deserved it.

The effects of cognitive dissonance are far-reaching. It creates a cloud of confusion, making it difficult to see the situation clearly. Rationalizing the abuser's behaviour becomes a coping mechanism. You might tell yourself that their hurtful comments are just "tough love" or that their moments of affection negate the abuse. This rationalization can make decision-making about the relationship incredibly challenging. You find yourself stuck in a loop, unable to break free because the mixed signals and conflicting emotions keep you tethered. The constant mental conflict leads to emotional exhaustion as you try to reconcile these opposing truths.

Consider a scenario where you receive a hurtful comment from your partner, which profoundly wounds you. Instead of confronting them, you might justify it by thinking, "They are just stressed; they didn't mean it."

Another example is believing that the occasional affectionate moments, like an unexpected gift or a rare apology, somehow cancel out the regular emotional abuse. These justifications keep you trapped, blurring the lines between acceptable and unacceptable behaviour.

Resolving cognitive dissonance requires deliberate effort. One effective method is reality-checking exercises. These involve documenting specific incidents of abuse and comparing them to the narcissist's words or actions during their affectionate moments. This practice helps you see the inconsistencies and recognize patterns of manipulation. Journaling conflicting thoughts can also bring clarity. By writing down your experiences and emotions, you can better understand the internal conflict and begin to separate reality from the abuser's distortions. Seeking external validation from trusted friends or family members can provide an objective perspective. Their insights can help you see the situation more clearly and reinforce the truth of your experiences.

2.4 Trauma Bonding: Why Leaving Feels Impossible

Trauma bonding is a psychological phenomenon where strong emotional attachments form between an abuser and their victim due to cycles of abuse and intermittent positive reinforcement. It's akin to emotional addiction, where your brain becomes hooked on the highs and lows of the relationship. These bonds are forged through the cycle of reward and punishment, making it incredibly difficult to leave the abuser. The intermittent reinforcement of affection and cruelty creates a deep psychological dependency, as your emotional needs are sporadically met, keeping you constantly off-balance and yearning for the next moment of kindness.

The mechanisms behind trauma bonding are complex. The cycle of reward and punishment plays a significant role. During the "good" times, the abuser fulfills your emotional needs, creating a sense of attachment and dependence. These moments of affection and kindness are powerful, starkly contrasting the periods of abuse. The abuser's role in fulfilling your emotional needs during these brief intervals strengthens the bond, making you more likely to stay despite the abuse. Shared experiences and history also contribute to this bond. The memories of happier times, even if few and far between, create a sense of connection that is hard to sever.

Trauma bonding complicates decision-making significantly. The fear of loneliness and abandonment looms, making the prospect of leaving seem impossible. Even when you recognize the abuse, the intermittent positive behaviours from the abuser create a glimmer of hope that things might change. You find yourself rationalizing staying, convinced that the abuser will revert to the loving person you once knew. This hope for change and redemption keeps you anchored in the toxic relationship, despite the ongoing harm.

Breaking free from trauma bonds requires a multifaceted approach. Gradual detachment and emotional distancing are critical first steps. This might involve reducing contact with the abuser, seeking safe spaces, and surrounding yourself with supportive individuals. Building a robust support network of friends and family can provide the emotional and practical support needed to break free. Professional counselling focused on trauma recovery can offer specialized strategies and coping mechanisms. Therapists trained in dealing with trauma bonds can help you understand the psychological dynamics at play and guide you through the process of emotional detachment.

Building self-awareness is another crucial aspect of breaking trauma bonds. Recognizing and acknowledging the bond is the first step toward dismantling it. This involves understanding the psychological mechanisms at play and accepting that the bond is based on trauma, not genuine attachment. Gradual detachment might mean slowly reducing interactions with the abuser, creating physical and emotional space, and focusing on self-care and personal growth. Emotional distancing can be facilitated by engaging in activities that promote independence and self-reliance, such as pursuing hobbies, learning new skills, and setting personal goals.

In conclusion, cognitive dissonance and trauma bonding are powerful forces that keep victims trapped in abusive relationships. The psychological conflict of holding contradictory beliefs creates confusion and emotional turmoil, while the deep emotional bonds formed through cycles of abuse and intermittent reinforcement make leaving feel impossible. However, by understanding these dynamics and employing practical strategies such as reality-checking exercises, journaling, seeking external validation, and building a support network, you can begin to break free from these bonds and reclaim your life. As we continue to explore the impact of narcissistic abuse, we will delve into the specific challenges of co-parenting with a narcissist and the importance of setting boundaries and protecting children.

Chapter 3: Practical Strategies for Immediate Relief

Imagine standing in a room filled with mirrors, each reflecting a distorted version of yourself. You see fragments, exaggerated and twisted, making it hard to recognize your true self. This is what it's like living under the constant scrutiny and manipulation of a narcissist. The reflections they show you are designed to confuse and control. But there is a way to shatter those mirrors and reclaim your reality. One of the most powerful tools you can use is the *No Contact Rule*.

3.1 The No Contact Rule: Cutting Ties Safely

The *No Contact Rule* is your lifeline. It means completely cutting off all communication with the narcissist. Why is this so crucial? First, it eliminates the narcissist's influence over you. As long as they have any means to contact you, they can continue their manipulation, keeping you trapped in a cycle of doubt and confusion. By cutting them off, you create a barrier that protects you from their toxic tactics. It also allows for emotional and psychological distance. Without their constant presence, you can start to see things more clearly, regaining a sense of normalcy and peace. Most importantly, it prevents further manipulation or abuse. Narcissists thrive on control. When you go to *No Contact*, you take back your power, denying them the opportunity to continue their harmful behaviour.

Implementing the *No Contact Rule* requires determination and meticulous planning. Start by blocking their phone numbers and social media accounts. This might seem drastic, but it's necessary. Any form of communication can be a gateway to worm their way back into your life. Inform mutual friends and family of your decision. Explain that you need their support in this, and ask them not to relay any messages from the narcissist. Changing routines and habits to avoid encounters is another critical step. If you frequent the same places, consider altering your schedule or finding new spots to spend your time. The goal is to minimize any chance of accidental meetings.

Maintaining *No Contact* can be challenging. Narcissists often try to re-enter your life through "hoovering" attempts. They might send you sweet messages, apologies, or even gifts to lure you back. Remember, these gestures are not sincere; they are strategies to regain control. Stand firm and do not respond. Guilt and second-guessing your decision can also creep in. You might wonder if you're being too harsh or if there's a chance they've changed. Remind yourself why you chose *No Contact* in the first place. Keep a journal of the reasons and refer to it whenever you feel doubt.

Situations where *No Contact* is impossible, like co-parenting, require a different approach. In such cases, limit your interactions to the bare minimum and keep them strictly about the children. Use written communication like emails or parenting apps to document everything. This helps maintain boundaries and provides a record in case conflicts arise.

Consider the story of Sarah, a professional who decided to go No Contact with her narcissistic partner. Initially, she felt overwhelmed by guilt and doubt. But as she blocked his number and unfollowed him on social media, she began to feel a sense of relief. Over time, she noticed her self-confidence returning. She no longer second-guessed her decisions or felt the constant weight of his judgment.

Another example is Tom, who found peace and clarity after cutting ties with his narcissistic ex. He had been subjected to years of emotional manipulation, but once he implemented No Contact, he started to reclaim his sense of self. The absence of constant criticism allowed him to rebuild his life and focus on his own growth.

Interactive Element: No Contact Commitment Checklist

Reflect on your readiness to implement the *No Contact Rule*. Use the checklist below to evaluate your preparedness:

- *Block Communication*: Have you blocked their phone number and social media accounts?

- *Inform Your Circle*: Have you informed mutual friends and family of your decision?

- *Change Routines*: Have you planned changes to your daily routines to avoid encounters?

- *Prepare for Hoovering*: Do you have a plan to handle hoovering attempts without engaging?

- *Journal Your Reasons*: Have you documented the reasons for going No Contact to refer back to?

If you can check off these items, you are well on your way to breaking free from the narcissist's control. Remember, this is your time to heal and rebuild. Stay committed to the process and lean on your support system for strength.

The journey of going to *No Contact* is not easy, but it is one of the most empowering steps you can take. By eliminating the narcissist's influence, you open the door to healing and reclaiming your life. You are not alone in this; many have walked this path before you, finding peace and strength on the other side.

3.2 Grey Rock Method: Minimizing Interaction

The Grey Rock Method is a technique designed to make yourself as uninteresting and unresponsive as possible when dealing with a narcissist. The goal is to minimize interaction and reduce the narcissist's interest in you. By becoming boring and unengaging, you deprive them of the emotional reactions they crave. This method involves avoiding eye contact, giving short answers, and refraining from showing any emotional responses. Essentially, you become a "grey rock" in the landscape of their lives—unremarkable and uninteresting. This method is not about being rude or confrontational; it's about self-preservation and creating a barrier to protect your emotional well-being.

There are specific situations where the Grey Rock Method is particularly useful. If you must interact with a narcissist at work, maintaining a professional but detached demeanour can help you navigate the relationship without giving them any emotional fuel. The same applies to co-parenting scenarios. When discussing matters related to your children, keep the conversations short and focused solely on the logistics. Avoid diving into personal topics that can give the narcissist an opening to manipulate you. Shared social circles or family gatherings can also be challenging. In these settings, use the Grey Rock Method to maintain a surface-level interaction, steering clear of deep or emotionally charged conversations.

Implementing the Grey Rock Method requires practical steps to be effective. Start by keeping all conversations short and factual. Stick to the basics and avoid elaborating on your thoughts or feelings. For example, a simple "It was fine" suffices if the narcissist asks how your day was. Avoid eye contact as much as possible, as it can be a conduit for emotional connection. Instead, focus on neutral points in the room or your tasks at hand. Practicing neutral and non-reactive body language is also crucial. Keep your expressions flat and your tone monotone. The less emotion you show, the less ammunition the narcissist has to use against you.

However, the Grey Rock Method has its downsides. One potential risk is the narcissist escalating their behaviour in an attempt to provoke a reaction from you. If this happens, ensure your safety first and foremost. Have a plan in place to remove yourself from the situation if things become too tense. Balancing between being unresponsive and maintaining necessary communication can also be tricky. You still need to communicate effectively, especially in professional or co-parenting scenarios. Stick to the facts and avoid any emotional engagement. Recognizing when to switch to *No Contact* if Grey Rock becomes ineffective is also important. If you find that the narcissist is still finding ways to manipulate or control you, consider cutting off all contact.

Interactive Element: Grey Rock Practice Script

To help you get started with the Grey Rock Method, here's a simple script you can follow:

Narcissist: "How was your weekend?" You: "It was fine, thank you." Narcissist: "What did you do?" You: "Just some chores and errands." Narcissist: "Anything exciting?" You: "No, just the usual."

By keeping your responses short and to the point, you minimize the opportunity for the narcissist to engage you in a manipulative conversation.

Using the Grey Rock Method can feel emotionally and mentally draining at times. It takes practice to maintain a neutral façade, especially when dealing with someone who knows exactly how to push your buttons. It's essential to have a support system in place, whether it's friends, family, or a therapist, to help you navigate the emotional toll. Regular self-care practices, like mindfulness or journaling, can also help you manage stress and maintain your emotional health. Remember, the goal is not to win or change the narcissist but to protect yourself and maintain your peace of mind.

3.3 Techniques for Self-Validation and Reality-Checking

Navigating life after experiencing narcissistic abuse often feels like walking through a dense fog, where your perceptions are constantly called into question. This is where self-validation becomes a lifeline. Self-validation is crucial for rebuilding trust in your own perceptions. When you've repeatedly been told that your feelings and experiences are wrong or exaggerated, it's easy to lose faith in your judgment. Self-validation helps you reclaim that trust, acting as a countermeasure to the gaslighting tactics often employed by narcissists. By acknowledging and accepting your emotions and experiences as valid, you start to rebuild your self-worth and confidence, laying the foundation for a stronger, more resilient self.

One of the most effective ways to practice self-validation is by keeping a journal of your daily experiences and emotions. Writing down what you go through each day helps solidify your reality. It serves as a concrete record that you can refer back to, especially on days when doubt creeps in. Alongside journaling, using affirmation statements can reinforce your belief in yourself. Simple affirmations like "My feelings are valid" or "I trust my perceptions" can be powerful tools. Visualization techniques also play a crucial role. Imagine a scenario where you stand firm in your truth, unaffected by external manipulations. Visualizing yourself in such situations can help you internalize these affirmations and make them a part of your daily mindset.

Reality-checking methods are another essential tool in your recovery toolkit. When a narcissist has muddied your sense of reality, seeking feedback from trusted friends or therapists can provide the clarity you need. These external perspectives can help you distinguish between what is real and what has been distorted by the narcissist. Comparing past and present behaviours of the narcissist can also be enlightening. Documenting these behaviours over time reveals patterns that are hard to ignore. Consistency is vital to seeing through the manipulations. Analyzing these patterns helps you understand the cyclical nature of their tactics, making it easier to anticipate and counteract them.

Consider the story of a woman who documented her experiences to counter the gaslighting she endured from her narcissistic partner. Each time he told her she was imagining things, she would refer to her journal, which detailed specific incidents and her feelings at the time. This practice helped her see the truth of her experiences, gradually rebuilding her confidence. Another individual used daily affirmations to combat the negative self-talk instilled by years of emotional abuse. By repeating phrases like "I am enough" and "I deserve respect," he slowly began to see himself in a more positive light, eventually regaining his self-esteem.

Interactive Element: Daily Self-Validation Exercise

Set aside a few minutes each day to complete this exercise:

- *Journal Entry*: Write down one significant event from your day and how it made you feel. Describe the event in detail.

- *Affirmation*: Choose an affirmation that resonates with you, write it down three times, and say it out loud to yourself.

- *Visualization*: Spend a moment visualizing a scenario where you stand firm in your truth. See yourself confident and unaffected by the narcissist's tactics.

This exercise can help solidify your perceptions and reinforce your self-belief, providing a daily anchor of reality and self-worth.

Self-validation and reality-checking are not just exercises; they are lifelines that keep you grounded in your truth. They help you navigate the murky waters of narcissistic abuse, providing clarity and reinforcing your sense of self. Each time you validate your experiences and check the reality against the narcissist's manipulations, you reclaim a piece of your identity. It's a gradual process, but with each step, you move closer to a life where you are in control of your reality.

3.4 Emergency Self-Care Routines

In moments of crisis, when the emotional weight feels unbearable, immediate self-care strategies can make all the difference. Mindfulness techniques and breathing exercises are invaluable tools. Simple practices like deep breathing can help calm your nervous system. Inhale slowly for a count of four, hold for four, and then exhale for four. Repeat this process until you feel a sense of calm wash over you. Mindfulness techniques, like focusing on the present moment, can also help ground you. Pay attention to your surroundings, and notice the sounds, the smells, and the textures. This shift in focus can provide a respite from overwhelming emotions.

Creating a safe and calming environment can offer immediate relief. Find a space in your home where you feel secure and at peace. This could be a cozy corner with a comfortable chair and soft lighting or a quiet room where you can close the door and shut out the world. Use this space to retreat when you need to decompress. Fill it with items that bring you comfort, like soft blankets, pillows, or even a favourite book. Temporary distractions, such as listening to music or engaging in hobbies, can also be effective. Music has a powerful ability to shift your mood. Create a playlist of songs that make you feel happy or relaxed. Hobbies, whether drawing, knitting, or even simple puzzles, can provide a mental break and help redirect your focus.

Developing a personalized self-care plan tailored to your specific needs and triggers is crucial for long-term well-being. Start by identifying your personal stressors. What are the situations or interactions that tend to overwhelm you? Once you have a clear understanding of your triggers, you can develop coping mechanisms to address them. For instance, if social interactions are a significant stressor, plan for regular alone time to recharge. Scheduling regular self-care activities is another important step. Make self-care a non-negotiable part of your routine. Whether it's a daily walk, a weekly yoga class, or a monthly spa day, having these activities on your calendar ensures you prioritize your well-being. Establishing a support network of friends and family can provide invaluable emotional support. Reach out to trusted individuals who can offer a listening ear or a comforting presence when you need it most.

An emergency self-care toolkit can be a lifesaver in times of acute stress. Consider including soothing scents or essential oils in your toolkit. Lavender, chamomile, and eucalyptus are known for their calming properties. A few drops on a handkerchief or in a diffuser can create a serene atmosphere. Comfort items like blankets or stuffed animals can also provide a sense of security. Having a contact list of supportive friends or hotlines is essential. Sometimes, just knowing you have someone to call can be comforting. Make sure this list is easily accessible, whether it's stored in your phone or written down in a notebook you keep nearby.

Real-life examples highlight the effectiveness of these strategies. Take the story of Jane, a survivor who used mindfulness to manage panic attacks. Whenever she felt an attack coming on, she would retreat to her safe space, light a lavender-scented candle, and focus on her breathing. This routine helped her regain control and calm her mind. Another example is Mark, who created a calming space in his home. He filled it with items that brought him peace, like a soft blanket, his favourite books, and a playlist of soothing music. Whenever he felt overwhelmed, he would spend time in this space, allowing himself to decompress and find clarity.

Emergency self-care routines are not just about immediate relief; they are about reclaiming control and stability in your life. With these strategies in place, you can navigate moments of crisis with greater ease and resilience. Remember, self-care is not a luxury; it is a necessity, especially when dealing with the aftermath of narcissistic abuse. Take the time to develop and refine your self-care routines, and trust that each small step you take is a step toward healing and empowerment.

As we move forward, we will explore the critical aspect of co-parenting with a narcissist and the strategies you can employ to protect your children and maintain your peace. This next chapter will delve into the unique challenges you face and offer practical solutions to navigate this complex dynamic.

Chapter 4: Rebuilding Self-Esteem

Imagine standing in front of a mirror and struggling to recognize the person staring back at you. The reflection seems fragmented, a collection of negative labels and doubts imposed by years of manipulation. This is the reality for many who have endured narcissistic abuse. Rebuilding self-esteem is not just about seeing a better reflection; it's about reclaiming your true self. One powerful tool in this journey is the practice of daily affirmations.

4.1 Affirmations and Daily Self-Love Practices

Affirmations are more than just positive statements; they are a way to reprogram your mind and rebuild your self-belief. The science behind affirmations is rooted in neuroplasticity, the brain's ability to reorganize itself by forming new neural connections. When you consistently repeat affirmations, you activate brain regions associated with self-processing and reward. This neural activity helps shift your focus towards positive self-worth and reduces your reactivity to negative thoughts. In essence, -

affirmations help you carve new mental pathways that foster a healthier self-image.

Consider the affirmation, "I am worthy of love and respect." Repeating this phrase daily can help counteract the negative self-beliefs instilled by a narcissist. Another powerful affirmation is, "I am capable and strong." This reminds you of your inherent abilities and resilience. These statements might initially feel strange or uncomfortable, but their power lies in repetition. Over time, they become ingrained in your subconscious, slowly transforming your self-perception.

Creating personalized affirmations can make this practice even more effective. Tailor your affirmations to address your specific needs and goals. Focus on your positive traits and achievements. For instance, if you've always been a caring friend, an affirmation like "I am a kind and compassionate person" can reinforce this quality. Use present tense and positive language to make the affirmation feel more immediate and real. Avoid negative words, even if you're trying to counter a negative belief. Instead of saying, "I am not weak," say, "I am strong." The goal is to create a positive mental image that your mind can latch onto.

Incorporating affirmations into your daily routine helps solidify their impact. Start your day by reciting affirmations during your morning routine. As you brush your teeth or make your coffee, say your affirmations out loud. This sets a positive tone for the day. Using affirmation cards or apps can also be helpful. Write your affirmations on small cards and place them where you'll see them often, like on your bathroom mirror or in your wallet. Several apps are designed to send you reminder notifications throughout the day, ensuring that your affirmations are always front and center. Writing affirmations on mirrors or sticky notes is another practical tip. Regularly seeing these positive statements can reinforce their message and keep you focused on self-improvement.

Real-life success stories illustrate the transformative power of affirmations. Take the case of Maria, who struggled with self-doubt after leaving an abusive relationship. She started using daily affirmations to rebuild her confidence. She would look in the mirror every morning and say, "I deserve happiness and success." Over time, these words began to resonate deeply within her. She noticed a shift in how she viewed herself and her capabilities. Maria started pursuing opportunities she once thought were out of reach, and her newfound confidence propelled her to new heights in both her personal and professional life.

Another example is John, who had lost his sense of self-worth due to years of emotional manipulation. He began a practice of repeating affirmations like, "I trust my judgment and decisions," and "I am enough, just as I am." These affirmations helped him quiet the inner critic that had been fueled by his abuser's words. John found that his confidence grew with each passing day. He was able to make decisions with greater clarity and conviction, ultimately leading him to a place of self-assurance and inner peace.

Interactive Element: Affirmation Creation Exercise

Take a moment to create your own personalized affirmations. Use the guidelines below to craft statements that resonate with you:

- *Identify a Negative Belief*: What is your negative belief about yourself?

- *Reframe into a Positive Statement*: Turn that negative belief into a positive affirmation.

- *Use Present Tense and Positive Language*: Ensure your affirmation uses positive language and is in the present tense.

Write down your affirmations and place them somewhere you'll see them daily. Repeat them regularly and watch as your self-esteem begins to transform.

Affirmations are powerful tools for rebuilding self-esteem. By consistently practicing positive self-talk, you can rewire your brain to focus on both your strengths and inherent worth. The journey to self-love and confidence may be challenging, but with each repetition, you pave the way for a more empowered and resilient self.

4.2 Journaling for Self-Discovery

Journaling is an incredible tool for self-discovery, offering a space to explore your thoughts, emotions, and experiences in a way that fosters deeper understanding and healing. When you put pen to paper, you allow yourself a moment of reflection, a chance to step back from the chaos and see things more clearly. This practice enhances self-awareness, helping you recognize patterns in your behaviour and identify triggers that might be contributing to your emotional state. By regularly journaling, you create a narrative of your life that you can revisit, giving you insights into how you've grown and changed over time.

Different journaling techniques can help you explore your inner self from various angles. Stream-of-consciousness writing is a method where you allow your thoughts to flow freely while you write without any specific structure or agenda. This technique can be incredibly liberating, as it lets you tap into your subconscious mind and uncover hidden emotions and ideas. Prompt-based journaling offers a more guided approach, where you respond to specific questions or topics. This can be particularly helpful if you need help figuring out where to start or want to focus on specific aspects of your life. Gratitude journaling is another powerful technique. By writing down things you're grateful for each day, you shift your focus from what's lacking to what's abundant in your life, fostering a more positive outlook.

Establishing a consistent journaling habit might seem daunting initially, but with a few practical tips, it can become a rewarding part of your daily routine. Start by setting aside a dedicated time each day for journaling. It doesn't have to be long—even ten minutes can make a difference. Choose a time when you're least likely to be interrupted, like early in the morning or right before bed. Creating a comfortable journaling space is also important. Find a quiet spot where you can relax and focus, whether it's a cozy corner of your home or a favourite café. Make this space inviting with soft lighting, comfortable seating, and perhaps some calming music. Your first decision will be whether you prefer a digital or physical journal. Some people love the tactile experience of writing by hand, while others find it easier to type on a computer or use a journaling app.

Journaling for self-discovery doesn't just help you understand yourself better; it also provides a safe space to process and release emotions. For example, Sarah found solace in stream-of-consciousness writing after her divorce. She discovered patterns in her emotions and behaviours that she hadn't noticed before, which helped her make more informed decisions about her future. John used gratitude journaling to combat feelings of depression. By writing down three things he was grateful for each day, he gradually shifted his focus from negative thoughts to positive aspects of his life, improving his overall mood and outlook.

Interactive Element: Journaling Prompt Exercise

To help you get started, here are some specific prompts that can guide your journaling journey. Try this exercise to kickstart your journaling practice. Choose one of the following prompts and write for at least ten minutes without stopping:

- "What are three things you love about yourself?"
- "Describe a time when you overcame a challenge."
- "List five positive qualities you admire in yourself."

Don't worry about grammar or punctuation. Just let your thoughts flow and see where they take you.

Integrating journaling into your daily routine can be a transformative experience. It offers a private sanctuary to explore your innermost thoughts and feelings, uncover hidden insights, and track your personal growth. Consistency is key whether you choose stream-of-consciousness writing, prompt-based journaling, or gratitude journaling. Set aside time each day to write, create a comfortable space, and use prompts to guide your reflections. As you continue this practice, you'll find that journaling enhances your self-awareness and provides a powerful tool for healing and personal growth.

4.3 Reconnecting with Your Inner Strength

Reconnecting with your inner strength starts with recognizing and acknowledging the resilience that's already within you. It's easy to feel lost and powerless after enduring narcissistic abuse, but you have survived, and that in itself is a testament to your strength. Begin by reflecting on your past achievements and challenges. Think about moments when you overcame obstacles or achieved something significant. These moments are proof of your capabilities and resilience. Write them down and reflect on how you succeeded despite the difficulties. This practice helps you see the strength you have always had, even if it was overshadowed by the abuse.

Seeking feedback from trusted friends and family can also provide valuable insights into your strengths. Sometimes, those closest to us can see qualities that we might overlook or undervalue. Ask them about times when they saw you at your best. What qualities did you exhibit? What strengths did you show? Their perspectives can offer a more rounded view of your abilities and reinforce your self-belief. It's important to choose supportive people who have your best interests at heart, as their feedback will be both honest and encouraging.

Once you've identified your strengths, the next step is to build on them. Setting goals that align with your strengths can provide a sense of direction and purpose. For instance, if you've identified that you have strong problem-solving skills, set a goal that allows you to use this strength, such as tackling a complex project at work or solving a challenging puzzle. Engaging in activities that leverage your talents boosts your confidence and gives you a sense of accomplishment. Whether it's a hobby, a job, or a volunteer activity, find ways to incorporate your strengths into your daily life. This continuous practice will help solidify these strengths and make them an integral part of who you are.

Developing new skills and competencies is another way to reconnect with your inner strength. Exploring new interests can be incredibly empowering. Take up a new hobby or enroll in a class that piques your interest. Whether it's learning a new language, picking up a musical instrument, or trying your hand at painting, these activities can open up new avenues for personal growth. Volunteering or participating in community activities can also provide opportunities to develop new skills while giving back to your community. These experiences enhance your skill set and connect you with others, fostering a sense of belonging and purpose.

Consider the story of Lisa, a survivor who pursued a new career path after leaving an abusive relationship. She was always passionate about helping others but needed more confidence to pursue it professionally. After recognizing her strength and resilience, she enrolled in a social work program. The journey was challenging, but each step reinforced her belief in her abilities. Today, Lisa is a licensed social worker, helping others overcome their own struggles. Her story is a powerful reminder that it's never too late to follow your passions and that your inner strength can guide you to new, fulfilling paths.

Another example is Mark, who developed a new passion for woodworking after his experience with narcissistic abuse. He found solace in creating something tangible with his hands, starkly contrasting the intangible emotional turmoil he had endured. Mark honed his skills through woodworking classes and community workshops and discovered a new talent. This newfound passion gave him a creative outlet and helped him reconnect with his inner strength. His sense of accomplishment with each completed project was a testament to his resilience and ability to rebuild his life on his own terms.

Reconnecting with your inner strength is a multifaceted process that involves recognizing your existing strengths, building on them, and developing new skills. It's about acknowledging your resilience and using it as a foundation to rebuild your life. By reflecting on past achievements, seeking feedback from supportive individuals, and exploring new interests, you can rediscover the strength that has always been within you.

4.4 Overcoming Shame and Embarrassment

Shame and embarrassment are often the silent companions of narcissistic abuse, lurking in the shadows and casting long, dark clouds over your sense of self. The roots of these feelings can be traced back to the constant criticism and belittling that characterize abusive relationships. When someone you trust and care about repeatedly tells you that you are not good enough, you start to internalize these negative messages. Over time, these harsh words become a part of your inner dialogue, shaping how you see yourself and your worth. This internalization is insidious, embedding itself deep within your psyche and making it difficult to see yourself in a positive light.

Challenging these deeply ingrained negative self-beliefs requires deliberate effort and practical strategies. One effective approach is to reframe negative thoughts. This involves recognizing when you are being self-critical and consciously shifting your perspective. For example, if you catch yourself thinking, "I'm a failure," pause and reframe it to, "I faced a difficult situation and did my best." This shift in perspective helps break the cycle of self-criticism and fosters a more compassionate view of yourself. Seeking validation from supportive individuals can also be incredibly healing. Surround yourself with friends and family who see your worth and value you for who you are. Their positive reinforcement can serve as a counterbalance to the negative messages you've internalized.

Practicing self-compassion is another vital step in overcoming shame and embarrassment. Self-compassion is treating yourself with the same kindness and understanding that you would offer to a friend. One technique for self-compassionate self-talk is to use phrases that acknowledge your struggles while offering comfort. For instance, saying, "It's okay to feel this way; I'm doing the best I can," can provide immediate relief and reassurance. Exercises for practicing self-forgiveness are also crucial. Write a letter to yourself, acknowledging the pain and struggle you've endured and expressing forgiveness for any perceived shortcomings. This act of self-forgiveness can be a powerful step towards healing and self-acceptance.

Real-life stories of individuals who have successfully overcome feelings of shame and embarrassment can provide inspiration and hope. Consider the story of Alex, who grew up with a narcissistic parent who constantly belittled his achievements. Alex felt ashamed of his accomplishments for years, believing they were never good enough. It wasn't until he started challenging these negative beliefs and seeking validation from supportive friends that he began to see his true worth. By embracing his talents and acknowledging his efforts, Alex was able to reclaim his sense of self and pursue his passions with confidence.

Another powerful example is Emma, who found strength in sharing her story publicly. After years of feeling embarrassed about her abusive past, Emma decided to speak out and raise awareness about narcissistic abuse. By sharing her experiences, she inspired others and found a sense of liberation and empowerment. Despite past criticism, her decision to embrace her true self allowed her to move forward with a renewed sense of purpose and self-assurance.

Interactive Element: Self-Compassion Exercise

Try this exercise to practice self-compassion: Find a quiet space and take a few deep breaths. Imagine a close friend is going through a similar experience, and think about what you would say to comfort them. Now, say those same words to yourself. Write them down if it helps. Repeat this exercise whenever you feel overwhelmed by shame or embarrassment.

Understanding the roots of shame and embarrassment, challenging negative self-beliefs, and practicing self-compassion are crucial steps in rebuilding your self-esteem. By treating yourself with kindness and seeking validation from supportive individuals, you can begin to dismantle the negative messages instilled by narcissistic abuse. Real-life stories of overcoming shame serve as powerful reminders that you are not alone and that it is possible to reclaim your sense of self-worth.

In the next chapter, we will explore strategies for setting and maintaining boundaries, an essential skill for protecting your well-being and fostering healthy relationships.

Chapter 5: Setting and Maintaining Boundaries

Imagine walking through a bustling city without any traffic lights or signs. Chaos would ensue. Cars would collide, pedestrians would be at constant risk, and the overall flow would be disrupted. Boundaries function like traffic signals in our personal lives. They create order, ensure safety, and help navigate relationships smoothly. Setting and maintaining boundaries is crucial for protecting your well-being, especially after experiencing narcissistic abuse.

5.1 Identifying Your Limits

Understanding personal limits is the bedrock of setting effective boundaries. Recognizing and respecting your emotional, mental, and physical limits is essential for your well-being. These limits serve as a guide, helping you understand what you can handle and what you need to protect yourself from. You can also gain valuable insights by reflecting on your past experiences. Think about instances when you felt overwhelmed, stressed, or uncomfortable. What were the common factors in those situations? Identifying these triggers is the first step in understanding your limits.

Signs of stress and discomfort are your body signalling that a boundary has been crossed. Pay attention to physical symptoms like headaches, fatigue, or a racing heart. Mentally, you might feel anxious, irritable, or drained. Emotionally, you might experience feelings of resentment, guilt, or helplessness. Recognizing these signs can help you identify when your limits are being tested, allowing you to take action before reaching a breaking point.

Assessing your current boundaries involves thoroughly evaluating where you stand and where you need improvement. Start by journaling about recent boundary breaches. Write down specific incidents where you felt your boundaries were crossed. What happened? How did you feel? This exercise can help you identify patterns and pinpoint areas needing attention. Listing areas where you feel most vulnerable is another important step. Are there certain situations or people that consistently test your limits? Understanding these vulnerabilities can help you set more effective boundaries.

Setting clear, specific limits is crucial for protecting your well-being. Begin by creating a list of non-negotiables—things that are absolutely essential for your emotional, mental, and physical health. These could include needing time alone to recharge, not tolerating disrespectful behaviour, or ensuring your physical space is respected. Identifying acceptable and unacceptable behaviours is also key. Clearly define what behaviours you are willing to accept from others and what you are not. This clarity helps you communicate your boundaries more effectively. Setting boundaries around time and energy is equally important. Decide how much time and energy you are willing to invest in different relationships and activities. This helps prevent burnout and ensures you have enough resources for self-care.

Using self-reflection exercises can further refine your understanding of your needs and values. Writing prompts like "What makes me feel safe?" can help you identify the core elements contributing to your sense of security. Reflecting on these prompts can provide clarity and guide you in setting meaningful boundaries. Visualization exercises are another powerful tool. Close your eyes and envision a boundary-respecting environment. What does it look like? How do you feel in this space? This exercise can help you internalize what healthy boundaries look and feel like, making it easier to implement them in real life.

Seeking feedback from trusted friends or a therapist can offer valuable insights. Sometimes, an external perspective can highlight areas you might overlook. Discuss your boundaries with someone you trust and ask for their input. They might offer suggestions or point out patterns that you hadn't noticed. A therapist can provide professional guidance and help you navigate the complexities of setting and maintaining boundaries, especially if you're dealing with the aftermath of narcissistic abuse.

Interactive Element: Boundary Reflection Exercise

Take a moment to complete this exercise. Reflect on the following questions and write down your responses:

- What makes me feel safe?

- What are my non-negotiables?

- What behaviours am I willing to accept or not accept from others?

- How much time and energy am I willing to invest in different relationships and activities?

Use your responses to guide you in setting clear, specific boundaries that protect your well-being.

Identifying your limits is a crucial step in setting and maintaining effective boundaries. By understanding your emotional, mental, and physical limits, assessing your current boundaries, and setting clear, specific limits, you create a blueprint for protecting your well-being. Self-reflection exercises and seeking feedback from trusted individuals can refine your understanding and help you implement meaningful boundaries. This process empowers you to navigate relationships confidently and clearly, prioritizing your needs and well-being.

5.2 Communication Scripts for Boundary Setting

Clear communication is the backbone of setting and maintaining boundaries. It's not just about what you say but how you say it. Your tone and body language play significant roles in conveying your message. Imagine trying to set a boundary while mumbling or avoiding eye contact. Your words might be clear, but the delivery could undermine your intent. Assertive communication strikes a balance between being too passive, which can lead to your boundaries being ignored, and too aggressive, which can create unnecessary conflict. The key is to be firm yet respectful, ensuring your message is heard without escalating tensions.

Creating effective scripts for boundary setting can make these conversations less daunting. In personal relationships, you might say, "I need some alone time to recharge." This statement is straightforward and focuses on your needs without blaming or criticizing the other person. In professional settings, a script like, "I can't work late tonight due to prior commitments," clearly communicates your limits while maintaining professionalism. For social interactions, consider saying, "I prefer not to discuss this topic." This sets a boundary without inviting further debate. These scripts serve as templates you can adapt to fit various situations, ensuring you're prepared to confidently assert your needs.

Practicing assertiveness is crucial for building confidence in boundary setting. One effective method is role-playing scenarios with a friend. This practice allows you to simulate real-life situations in a safe environment, which gives you the opportunity to refine your delivery and receive constructive feedback. Recording and reviewing self-practice sessions can also be beneficial. By watching yourself, you can identify areas for improvement, such as adjusting your tone or body language. Joining assertiveness training workshops provides a structured setting to learn and practice these skills, often with the guidance of experienced trainers. These workshops can offer valuable insights and techniques you might need help discovering.

Handling pushback is an inevitable part of enforcing boundaries. Not everyone will respect your limits immediately, and some may even try to challenge them. Staying firm and reiterating your boundaries is essential. For example, calmly repeat your statement if someone continues to push after you've set a boundary. The "broken record" technique, where you consistently repeat your boundary without getting drawn into an argument, can be particularly effective. This method reinforces your stance without escalating the situation. Recognizing manipulative tactics is also crucial. Some individuals may use guilt, anger, or other strategies to make you question your boundaries. Standing your ground involves being aware of these tactics and staying committed to your limits.

Interactive Element: Boundary-Setting Practice Exercise

Take a moment to practice setting a boundary using the following script. Imagine you need to tell a friend that you can't lend them money:

- **Describe**: "I noticed you've asked to borrow money several times recently."

- **Express**: "I feel uncomfortable when I'm asked for money because it puts me in a difficult position."

- **Assert Needs**: "I won't be able to lend you money in the future."

- **Reinforce**: "This will help maintain our friendship without financial stress."

Practice saying this script aloud, focusing on a calm tone and confident body language.

By emphasizing clear communication, creating effective scripts, practicing assertiveness, and handling pushback, you equip yourself with the necessary tools to set and maintain boundaries confidently. These strategies protect your well-being and foster healthier, more respectful relationships.

5.3 Dealing with Boundary Violations

Recognizing boundary violations is crucial for maintaining your emotional and psychological well-being. When someone crosses your boundaries, you often feel it in your gut. You might experience feelings of being disrespected, stressed, or even anxious. These are clear signs that a boundary has been breached. For instance, if a friend repeatedly cancels plans at the last minute, you may feel undervalued and frustrated. The emotional and psychological impact of repeated violations can be profound. Over time, these breaches can erode your self-esteem and make you question your worth. You might start to feel helpless and trapped, believing that your boundaries aren't worth respecting.

Immediate response strategies are essential for addressing boundary violations as they occur. One effective approach is to calmly but firmly address the behaviour. Use "I" statements to express your feelings and set the tone for a constructive conversation. For example, you might say, "I feel disrespected when my time isn't taken into consideration." This shifts the focus to your experience rather than accusing the other person, which can help defuse potential defensiveness. If the violation is severe or you're feeling overwhelmed, temporarily removing yourself from the situation may be necessary. Taking a break allows you to gather your thoughts and emotions, ensuring you can address the issue from a place of calm rather than anger or hurt.

Setting consequences for boundary violations is a powerful way to reinforce your limits. It's not enough to simply state your boundaries; you must communicate the repercussions of crossing them. For instance, if a coworker invades your personal space despite your requests, you might limit your interactions with them to strictly professional matters. Clearly communicate these consequences. Let the person know, "If this continues, I will have to limit our interactions to work-related topics only." Following through consistently is key. If you set a consequence and fail to enforce it, your boundaries lose effectiveness. People need to understand that your limits are non-negotiable and that there are real repercussions for ignoring them.

Reevaluating and reinforcing boundaries after violations occur is an ongoing process. Reflect on the incident to understand what went wrong and how you can adjust your boundaries to prevent future breaches. Ask yourself, "Did I communicate my boundary clearly? Was the consequence appropriate?" Seeking support from friends, family, or a therapist can provide valuable insights and help you navigate the emotional fallout of boundary violations. They can offer different perspectives and practical advice, making adjusting and strengthening your boundaries easier. Practicing self-care to recover from boundary breaches is equally important. Engage in activities that restore your emotional and mental well-being, whether spending time in nature, practicing mindfulness, or indulging in a favourite hobby. Taking care of yourself ensures you have the resilience and strength to maintain your boundaries in the future.

5.4 Maintaining Boundaries in Co-Parenting

Establishing co-parenting boundaries when dealing with a narcissistic ex-partner is a critical task. It's about creating a structure that protects your well-being and ensures a stable environment for your children. Setting communication guidelines is the first step. Designate specific times for discussions related to your child. This can prevent constant interruptions and reduce the likelihood of emotionally charged conversations. For example, agree to discuss co-parenting issues only on Sunday evenings. This gives you time to prepare mentally and emotionally, setting the stage for a more controlled interaction.

Clearly defining roles and responsibilities can also mitigate conflicts. Specify who is responsible for what aspects of your child's life, such as medical appointments, school activities, and extracurricular events. When each parent knows their role, it reduces misunderstandings and provides a clear framework for both parties to follow. This clarity also helps the children understand what to expect, fostering a more predictable and secure environment.

Effective communication with a narcissistic co-parent requires a strategic approach. Using written communication, such as emails or parenting apps, can document interactions and provide a record of agreements. This helps keep conversations focused on the children and serves as evidence if disputes arise. Written communication also reduces opportunities for manipulation, specifically gaslighting. Keeping conversations strictly about the children is crucial. Avoid discussing personal matters or past grievances. Staying neutral and avoiding emotional triggers can prevent the narcissist from exploiting your emotions. For instance, if the conversation starts to veer off into personal attacks, gently steer it back to the topic at hand. This approach minimizes conflict and keeps the focus on what truly matters—the well-being of your children.

Handling boundary breaches by the co-parent requires a firm and consistent response. Documenting incidents of boundary violations is essential. Keep a detailed record of each breach's dates, times, and descriptions. This documentation can be invaluable if you seek mediation or legal advice. When a boundary is crossed, reaffirm your boundaries and the consequences with the co-parent. For example, if they repeatedly contact you outside the agreed-upon times, remind them of the communication guidelines and the reasons behind them. If necessary, escalate the issue by seeking mediation or legal intervention to enforce the boundaries and protect your well-being and that of your children.

Supporting children through boundary enforcement is just as important as setting the boundaries themselves. Communicate these boundaries to your children in an age-appropriate manner. Explain why specific rules are in place and how they help create a safe and stable environment. Encourage your children to express their feelings and needs. Let them know that their voices matter and that they can come to you with their concerns. Providing a stable and predictable environment helps children feel more secure. Consistency in routines and expectations can offer reassurance and reduce anxiety. For instance, maintaining regular meal times, bedtime routines, and weekend schedules can provide a sense of normalcy amidst the co-parenting dynamics.

Interactive Element: Co-Parenting Communication Plan

Create a communication plan with the following steps:

- *Designate Times*: Agree on specific times for discussions related to co-parenting.

- *Use Written Communication*: Utilize emails or parenting apps to document interactions.

- *Define Roles*: Clearly outline each parent's responsibilities regarding the child's activities and needs.

Implementing this plan can help maintain clear and respectful communication, reduce conflicts, and focus on the child's welfare.

You create a healthier co-parenting dynamic by setting clear boundaries, maintaining effective communication, handling breaches consistently, and supporting your children. These strategies not only protect your well-being but also ensure a stable and supportive environment for your children, helping them thrive despite the challenges of co-parenting with a narcissist.

In the next chapter, we will explore the process of rebuilding self-esteem, focusing on practical exercises and strategies to regain your confidence and sense of self-worth after experiencing narcissistic abuse.

Chapter 6: Navigating Relationships Post-Abuse

Imagine meeting someone new and feeling a flicker of hope. This could be the start of something beautiful. But as you move forward, those familiar feelings of doubt and fear creep in. How do you know if this time will be different? How can you trust that you won't fall into the same traps again? Navigating new relationships after experiencing narcissistic abuse is challenging, but it's also an opportunity to build healthier connections. Recognizing red flags early on is crucial in protecting yourself from repeating past mistakes.

6.1 Recognizing Red Flags in New Relationships

Spotting red flags early in a relationship can save you from heartache and emotional turmoil down the road. One of the most telling signs is overly controlling behaviour. Take note if your new partner insists on knowing where you are at all times, who you're with, or tries to dictate your choices. Control often starts subtly but can escalate rapidly, eroding your autonomy and self-esteem. Excessive jealousy or possessiveness is another significant red flag. While it's natural to feel a little jealous now and then, constant accusations or demands for reassurance can signal deeper issues of insecurity and control.

Inconsistent actions and words are also major warning signs. Pay attention to whether your partner's actions align with their words. If they promise to change but continue to exhibit the same harmful behaviours, it clearly indicates something is amiss. Similarly, if they say one thing but do another, it can create a sense of instability and mistrust. Isolation from friends and family is a classic tactic used by narcissists to gain control over their victims. If your partner discourages you from seeing loved ones or makes you feel guilty for spending time with them, recognize this as a serious red fl ag.

Healthy communication is the bedrock of any strong relationship. Frequent lying or deceit, even about seemingly minor things, clearly indicates dysfunctional communication. Trust is built on honesty, and if your partner can't be truthful, it's impossible to establish a solid foundation. Refusal to discuss feelings or issues is another significant concern. Open dialogue is essential for resolving conflicts and understanding each other's perspectives. If your partner shuts down, avoids conversations, or dismisses your feelings, it's a sign that they may not be willing to engage in a meaningful and healthy way.

Observing how a potential partner handles stress and conflict can reveal much about their character. Anger management issues, such as explosive outbursts or aggressive behaviour, are significant red flags. A partner who blames others for their problems rather than taking responsibility demonstrates a lack of accountability. This blame-shifting can create a toxic environment where you constantly feel at fault. An inability to apologize or take responsibility for mistakes further underscores a lack of maturity and emotional intelligence. A healthy relationship requires both partners to acknowledge their faults and work together to grow.

Trusting your instincts is perhaps one of the most vital lessons after surviving narcissistic abuse. Your gut feelings are often your subconscious picking up on subtle cues that your conscious mind might miss. If you feel a sense of unease or discomfort around your new partner, don't ignore it. These feelings are there for a reason and can serve as an early warning system. Noticing patterns similar to past abusive relationships is another critical aspect. If you see behaviours that remind you of your past abuser, even if they seem minor, it's essential to take them seriously.

Interactive Element: Red Flag Reflection Exercise

Take a moment to reflect on any past relationships. Write down any red flags you recognized in hindsight. Consider the following questions:

- Did your partner exhibit overly controlling behaviour?
- Were they excessively jealous or possessive?
- Did they isolate you from friends and family?
- Were their actions inconsistent with their words?
- How did they handle stress and conflict?
- Did you notice any patterns similar to your past abusive relationships?

Understanding these patterns can help you identify red flags earlier in future relationships, allowing you to protect yourself and make more informed choices.

Recognizing these red flags empowers you to navigate new relationships with greater awareness and caution. Remembering that you deserve a relationship built on trust, respect, and mutual understanding is crucial. By staying vigilant and trusting your instincts, you can create healthier and more fulfilling connections moving forward.

6.2 Building Healthy Relationships

Imagine stepping into a new relationship with a fresh perspective, armed with the wisdom you've gained from past experiences. The foundation of a healthy relationship is built on mutual respect and empathy. This means valuing each other's perspectives and feelings, even when they differ from your own. When both partners show genuine empathy, it creates a safe space where you can express yourself without fear of judgment. Mutual respect ensures that you both feel valued and appreciated, laying the groundwork for a supportive and loving connection.

Open and honest communication is another cornerstone of a healthy relationship. It's about more than just sharing your thoughts; it's about being transparent and forthcoming, even when the conversations are difficult. Sharing your feelings and being open about your needs creates a deeper level of intimacy and trust. When both partners are committed to honest dialogue, misunderstandings can be resolved more efficiently, and you can work through conflicts together. Shared values and goals are also crucial. Aligning on what matters most to both of you helps create a unified vision for your relationship. It could be as simple as agreeing on how to spend your weekends or as significant as planning your future together. These shared values act as a compass, guiding your relationship in a direction that feels right for both of you.

Equality in decision-making is vital. In a healthy relationship, both partners have an equal say. Whether deciding on major life choices or everyday decisions, feeling that your voice matters fosters a sense of partnership and collaboration. This balance ensures neither partner feels overpowered or marginalized, promoting a harmonious dynamic.

Creating strong communication habits is essential for maintaining a healthy relationship. Active listening techniques play a significant role here. This means fully focusing on your partner when they speak, showing that you value their words. Nodding, maintaining eye contact, and providing verbal affirmations like "I understand" can make your partner feel heard. Expressing your needs and desires clearly is equally important. Use "I" statements to communicate your feelings without sounding accusatory. For example, say, "I feel upset when plans change at the last minute," instead of, "You always change plans." This approach fosters understanding rather than defensiveness.

Conflict resolution skills are crucial for navigating disagreements. Aim to stay calm and focused on the issue at hand. Avoid bringing up past conflicts or resorting to personal attacks. Instead, try to understand your partner's perspective and find common ground. Regular check-ins with your partner can also help maintain a healthy communication flow. Set aside time to discuss how you both feel about the relationship, addressing any concerns before they escalate into more significant issues.

Establishing trust and transparency is another key aspect of a strong relationship. Being honest about past experiences, especially those that have shaped who you are, helps build a foundation of trust. When you share your history, it shows vulnerability and a willingness to be open. Setting expectations and boundaries early on is also essential. Discuss what you both need and expect from the relationship to ensure you're on the same page. Following through on promises reinforces trust. Consistency in your actions shows that you are reliable and dependable, which strengthens the bond between you.

Practicing emotional intelligence can transform the way you relate to your partner. Recognizing and managing your emotions is the first step. When you're aware of your feelings, you can communicate them more effectively. Empathizing with your partner's feelings is equally important. Trying to understand their emotions and responding with compassion creates a deeper connection and fosters mutual respect. Responding rather than reacting is another crucial skill. When conflicts arise, take a moment to process your emotions before responding. This approach helps you communicate more thoughtfully and avoid escalating the situation.

Building a healthy relationship after experiencing narcissistic abuse is about creating a space where both partners feel valued, respected, and heard. You can nurture a supportive and fulfilling connection by focusing on mutual respect, open communication, shared values, equality, trust, and emotional intelligence. It's about learning from the past and using that knowledge to build a brighter, healthier future with your partner.

6.3 Strategies for Trusting Again

Rebuilding trust after experiencing narcissistic abuse is a gradual process that can't be rushed. It's like healing a deep wound; it requires time, care, and patience. Allow yourself the time to heal. Understand that it's perfectly normal for trust to come back slowly. After all, you've been through a lot, and those emotional scars need time to mend. Patience with yourself is key. Recognize that progress is not always linear. You will have good days and bad days. Celebrate the small victories and understand that setbacks are part of the healing process. Trust grows in increments, not leaps.

Taking small, manageable steps can make the process less overwhelming. Start by sharing small personal details with new people in your life. This could be something as simple as your favourite book or a childhood memory. Observe how your partner responds to your needs. Do they listen attentively? Do they respect your feelings? Gradually increase your vulnerability as you become more comfortable. Start with sharing minor secrets, then move on to deeper, more personal information. Each positive interaction will help build your confidence. Celebrate these small victories in trust. Acknowledge moments when you felt heard and understood. These are the building blocks of a trusting relationship.

Seeking reassurance and validation from trusted sources is crucial. Talk to friends or family members who have your best interests at heart. Their support and perspective can help you see things more clearly. Consulting with a therapist can provide professional guidance and tools to help you rebuild trust. Therapists can help you navigate your emotions and provide strategies for dealing with trust issues. Joining support groups for survivors of narcissistic abuse can also be incredibly validating. Sharing your experiences with others who have gone through similar situations can provide comfort and understanding. These groups offer a safe space to express your feelings and receive support.

Trusting yourself first is the most important step in this process. After all, if you can't trust yourself, how can you trust others? Start by listening to your intuition. Your gut feelings are there for a reason. They are your internal alarm system designed to protect you. Pay attention to these feelings, especially when something doesn't feel right. Validating your own experiences and feelings is also essential. Don't let anyone make you doubt your reality. Your experiences are valid, and your feelings are real. Building confidence in your judgment takes time, but it's worth the effort. Each time you make a decision that turns out well, your confidence grows. Trust in your ability to navigate relationships will follow.

Imagine Sarah, who, after years of emotional manipulation, decided to take small steps towards trusting others. She started by sharing her favourite hobbies with a new friend and observed how they respected her interests. Over time, she felt more comfortable sharing deeper aspects of her life. Each positive response from her friend built her confidence. Meanwhile, John sought reassurance from his therapist and joined a support group. These steps helped him understand that his feelings were valid and that he wasn't alone in his experiences. He learned to trust his judgment and gradually opened up to new relationships.

Consider the visual element of a trust-building ladder. At the bottom rung, you start with simple, everyday interactions. As you climb, each rung represents deeper levels of sharing and vulnerability. The top of the ladder symbolizes a strong, trusting relationship. Each step up the ladder is a small victory in itself. This visual can help you see trust as a series of achievable steps rather than a daunting leap.

Rebuilding trust is not a destination but a continuous process. It requires taking small, manageable steps, seeking reassurance from trusted sources, and, most importantly, trusting yourself first. By allowing yourself the time to heal and being patient with the process, you can rebuild trust and open the door to healthy, fulfilling relationships.

6.4 Balancing Vulnerability and Protection

Healthy vulnerability is an essential aspect of building meaningful relationships. It's about openly sharing your feelings and experiences, allowing yourself to be seen and heard for who you truly are. When you let your guard down and show someone your authentic self, you create opportunities for deeper connections. This openness fosters trust and intimacy, which are the cornerstones of any strong relationship. Imagine sitting with a new partner and sharing a personal story or expressing your fears. This act of vulnerability can be incredibly bonding, as it shows your willingness to be genuine and authentic.

However, being vulnerable doesn't mean throwing caution to the wind. It's crucial to balance vulnerability with protective boundaries. One effective strategy is to share in stages rather than all at once. Start with small, less personal details and gradually reveal more as you feel comfortable and trust is built. This approach protects you and allows the relationship to develop naturally. Being selective about what you share initially is another important tactic. Gauge the other person's reactions and responses before diving into more sensitive topics. Clear communication about your needs and limits is also vital. Let your partner know what you're comfortable with and what areas are off-limits for now. This clarity helps set expectations and ensures that both parties feel respected and understood.

Recognizing when to pull back is equally important. Pay attention to your feelings of discomfort or unease when sharing. It might be a sign to slow down if you start to feel vulnerable or exposed. Observe your partner's reactions closely. Negative responses or red flags, such as dismissiveness or lack of empathy, are indicators that you might need to reassess the relationship dynamics. Trust your instincts in these moments. If something feels off, taking a step back and protecting yourself is better. Reassessing the relationship allows you to make informed decisions about your level of openness and engagement.

Balancing self-care with relationship care is another crucial aspect of navigating new relationships. While it's natural to want to invest time and energy into a new connection, it's essential to maintain sight of your own well-being. Ensure you have personal time and space to recharge. This might mean scheduling regular alone time or engaging in activities that bring you joy and relaxation. Prioritizing your emotional and mental well-being is key. Make self-care practices, such as mindfulness or exercise, a non-negotiable part of your routine. These activities help you stay grounded and resilient, enabling you to bring your best self to the relationship.

Maintaining your personal goals and interests is also vital. It's easy to get swept up in a new relationship and put your aspirations on the back burner. However, staying connected to your passions and goals keeps you balanced and fulfilled. Whether it's pursuing a hobby, advancing in your career, or spending time with friends, these activities nourish your sense of self. They remind you that you are a whole and complete person, both within and outside of your relationships.

Consider the story of Jane, who entered a new relationship after leaving an abusive one. She practiced sharing in stages, initially revealing small aspects of her life and gradually opening up as trust was built. She communicated her boundaries clearly, letting her partner know when she needed space or felt uncomfortable. She stepped back to reassess the situation when she noticed any signs of unease. Jane balanced her relationship care with self-care by continuing her yoga practice and spending time with friends. This approach allowed her to nurture a healthy relationship while maintaining her well-being.

Balancing vulnerability and protection creates a space for open and authentic expression while safeguarding emotional health. It's about finding that sweet spot where you feel seen and heard without feeling exposed or at risk. By setting clear boundaries, recognizing when to pull back, and prioritizing self-care, you can navigate new relationships with confidence and grace.

Make a Difference with Your Review

Unlock the Power of Generosity

"The best way to find yourself is to lose yourself in the service of others." - Mahatma Gandhi

People who give without expecting anything in return live happier lives. So, let's make a difference together!

Would you help someone just like you—curious about surviving narcissistic abuse but unsure where to start?

My mission is to make the journey of healing from narcissistic abuse easier and more hopeful for everyone.

But to reach more people, I need your help.

Most readers choose books based on reviews. So, I'm asking you to help a fellow survivor by leaving a review.

It costs nothing and takes less than a minute but could change someone's path to healing. Your review could help…

…one more person find their strength.

…one more heart feel understood.

…one more individual regain their confidence.

…one more soul discover hope.

…one more life transform for the better.

If you love helping others, you're my kind of person.

To make a difference, simply scan the QR code below and leave a review:

Thank you from the bottom of my heart!

K.C. Lockwood

Chapter 7: Legal and Safety Considerations

Imagine waking up one morning and realizing that enough is enough. The abuse, the manipulation, and the fear have taken their toll, and you're ready to take back control of your life. But where do you start? Navigating the legal landscape to protect yourself and your children can seem daunting. Understanding your legal rights and the steps you can take for protection are crucial in this journey toward safety and empowerment.

7.1 Legal Rights and Protection Orders

Understanding your legal rights is the first step in protecting yourself from further harm. As a survivor of domestic abuse, you are entitled to various legal protections designed to ensure your safety and well-being. These protections are not just limited to physical abuse but also cover psychological and emotional abuse, which can be equally damaging.

Domestic abuse is a crime, and you have the right to report your abuser to the authorities. In many places, laws have been enacted specifically to address the complexities of narcissistic and psychological abuse. For instance, in the UK, you can seek civil orders like Non-Molestation Orders or Restraining Orders without involving the police directly. These orders can provide immediate protection by legally prohibiting the abuser from contacting or approaching you.

If you have children, your rights extend to ensuring their safety and well-being as well. You can apply for **Child Arrangements Orders** through the family court to set terms for child contact, thereby protecting your children from being used as tools of manipulation. Understanding these rights empowers you to take the necessary steps to safeguard your family.

When considering protection orders, it's important to understand the different types available and their specific purposes. **Temporary Restraining Orders (TROs)** are often issued quickly to provide immediate protection while a more permanent solution is sought. These orders can prevent the abuser from contacting or approaching you for a specified period, usually until a court hearing can take place.

Permanent Restraining Orders offer longer-term protection and are issued after a court hearing where both parties can present their case. These orders can include various provisions, such as prohibiting contact, maintaining a certain distance from your residence, workplace, or children's school, and surrendering firearms if applicable.

No-Contact Orders are typically issued after a criminal charge and prohibit any form of contact between the abuser and the victim. This includes direct contact through phone calls, emails, and social media, as well as indirect contact through third parties. These orders are crucial in ensuring that the abuser cannot continue their manipulation and harassment.

Orders of Protection for children are specifically designed to safeguard minors from abusive behaviour. These orders can include provisions such as supervised visitation, restrictions on the abuser's presence at the child's school or daycare, and mandatory counselling for the abuser. Ensuring your children are protected is a vital part of breaking free from the cycle of abuse.

Obtaining a protection order involves several steps designed to ensure your case is heard and you receive the protection you need. The first step is gathering evidence to support your application. This can include text messages, emails, witness statements, and other documentation demonstrating the abuse. Keeping a detailed journal of incidents can also be invaluable, providing a clear record of the abuse over time.

Once you have gathered your evidence, you will need to file the necessary paperwork at your local court. This process can vary depending on your location, but court staff are usually available to guide you through the forms and procedures. After filing, you will be given a date for a court hearing where you can present your case. Attending this hearing and bringing all your evidence with you is essential. The judge will review the information and decide whether to grant the protection order.

Enforcing protection orders is crucial for ensuring your safety. If the abuser violates the terms of the order, it's important to report these violations to the authorities immediately. Keeping detailed records of all incidents, including dates, times, and descriptions of the violations, can strengthen your case if further legal action is needed. In some cases, seeking legal assistance may be necessary to enforce the order properly. Lawyers experienced in domestic abuse cases can provide valuable support and guidance, helping you navigate the legal system and advocating on your behalf.

Interactive Element: Protection Order Checklist

Creating a checklist can help you stay organized and ensure you cover all necessary steps when seeking a protection order:

- *Gather Evidence*: Collect text messages, emails, witness statements, and keep a detailed journal of incidents.

- *File Paperwork*: Complete and file the necessary forms at your local court.

- *Attend Hearing*: Present your case and evidence at the court hearing.

- *Enforce Order*: Report any violations to the authorities and keep detailed records of incidents.

Understanding your legal rights and knowing the steps to obtain and enforce protection orders can provide a sense of control and security. It's a vital part of taking back your power and ensuring your safety as you move forward.

7.2 Safety Planning for Leaving an Abusive Relationship

Creating a safety plan is like building a lifeline. It's a comprehensive strategy to ensure your safety and your children's. The first step is assessing immediate risks and needs. Take a moment to reflect on the specific threats you face. Is the abuser prone to physical violence? Do they have access to weapons? Understanding these risks helps you prioritize your actions. Identify safe places to go in an emergency. This could be a trusted friend's house, a family member's home, or a local shelter. Knowing where you can seek refuge provides a sense of security and a clear course of action when things escalate.

Preparing for departure involves meticulous planning. Start by packing an emergency bag with essentials. Include clothing, toiletries, medications, and any necessary supplies for your children. This bag should be easily accessible yet hidden from the abuser. Securing important documents is crucial. Gather IDs, birth certificates, financial records, and legal documents such as restraining orders. Keep these documents in a safe place, possibly within your emergency bag. Arranging transportation and safe housing is the next step. Plan how you will leave and where you will go. This might involve coordinating with friends or family who can offer a place to stay, or researching local shelters that provide temporary housing. Ensure you have a reliable means of transportation, whether it's your own vehicle, a taxi service, or public transit.

Seeking support and resources is vital for both your emotional and logistical needs. Reach out to domestic violence hotlines for immediate assistance and guidance. These hotlines can connect you with local resources, shelters, and support groups. Inform trusted friends or family members of your plan. Having a support network provides emotional strength and practical assistance. They can offer a safe place to stay, help you pack, or even provide transportation. Don't hesitate to lean on these trusted individuals; their support can make a significant difference.

Post-departure safety measures are essential to maintain your security after leaving the abusive relationship. One of the first steps is changing locks and securing your home. This prevents the abuser from gaining access to your new safe space. Consider installing additional security measures like cameras or alarm systems for added protection. Updating privacy settings on social media is also crucial. Ensure that your accounts are private and that location services are turned off. Be cautious about what you share online and who you connect with. Establishing a code word with trusted individuals for emergencies can be a lifesaver. This code word signals that you need immediate help without alerting the abuser. Share this code word with friends, family, and neighbours who can act quickly if you are in danger.

Interactive Element: Emergency Bag Checklist

Creating an emergency bag is a critical part of your safety plan. Use the checklist below to ensure you have all necessary items packed and ready:

- *Clothing*: Enough for a few days, including comfortable shoes.

- *Toiletries*: Toothbrush, toothpaste, soap, feminine hygiene products.

- *Medications*: Prescription medications and a list of any medical conditions or allergies.

- *Important Documents*: IDs, birth certificates, financial records, legal documents.

- *Cash and Credit Cards*: Have some cash and a spare credit card for emergencies.

- *Keys*: Spare keys to your home, car, and other important places.

- *Children's Essentials*: Clothing, diapers, formula, toys, and any comfort items.

Keep this bag hidden yet easily accessible, ready to grab at a moment's notice.

Leaving an abusive relationship is a monumental step, and having a detailed safety plan can make all the difference. By assessing immediate risks, preparing for departure, seeking support, and taking post-departure safety measures, you create a framework that prioritizes your well-being and that of your children. This plan serves as both a guide and a source of empowerment, reminding you that safety and freedom are within reach.

7.3 Navigating Custody Battles with a Narcissist

Navigating custody battles with a narcissist adds another layer of complexity to an already difficult situation. Understanding custody laws is crucial to ensure you are well-prepared and know what to expect. Custody can be categorized into different types: legal, physical, joint, and sole custody.

- *Legal custody*: the right to make important decisions about your child's life, such as education, healthcare, and religious upbringing.

- *Physical custody*: determines where the child will live.

- *Joint custody*: both parents share these responsibilities.

- *Sole custody*: grants these rights to one parent exclusively.

Courts consider several factors when making custody decisions, including the child's best interests, the parents' ability to cooperate, and any history of neglect or abuse. Demonstrating that you can provide a stable, loving environment is key to securing a favourable outcome.

Documenting the narcissist's abusive behaviour is essential for custody hearings. Keeping a detailed journal of incidents can provide a clear timeline and context for the court. Note dates, times, and specific behaviours or statements that reflect the abusive pattern. Collecting evidence, such as emails, texts, and witness statements, can further support your claims. Record any threats, manipulations, or abusive interactions. This evidence can be pivotal in demonstrating the narcissist's harmful behaviour and its impact on your children. Consistent documentation paints a comprehensive picture, helping the court understand the seriousness of the situation.

Working with legal professionals experienced in high-conflict custody battles is crucial. Finding a lawyer who understands narcissistic abuse can make a significant difference. Start by researching lawyers who specialize in family law and have experience with cases involving narcissistic ex-partners. Preparing for consultations is important; bring all your documented evidence and be ready to discuss your case in detail. Collaborating with your lawyer to build a strong case involves regular communication and transparency. Your lawyer can guide you on the best strategies to present your evidence and advocate for your children's best interests.

Managing interactions during custody exchanges with a narcissist requires careful planning to minimize conflict and ensure safety. Using neutral locations for exchanges can reduce the likelihood of confrontations. Public places like police stations or community centers provide a level of oversight that can deter abusive behaviour. Having a third party present during exchanges can also provide a buffer and witness to the interactions. This third party could be a trusted friend, family member, or professional supervised visitation service. Communicating through a parenting app can help maintain a record of all communications and reduce direct contact. Apps like OurFamilyWizard or TalkingParents are designed to facilitate co-parenting communication while keeping everything documented. These tools can help ensure that all interactions remain focused on the children and prevent the narcissist from using communication as a means to manipulate or harass you.

Navigating custody battles with a narcissist is undoubtedly challenging, but understanding custody laws, documenting abusive behaviour, working with experienced legal professionals, and managing interactions carefully can help you protect your children and secure a stable, loving environment for them.

7.4 Financial Independence and Planning

Taking control of your finances is crucial to regaining your independence and stability. Assessing your current financial situation is the first move. Start by listing all your assets and liabilities. This includes any bank accounts, properties, vehicles, and valuables you own. On the liability side, jot down any debts, loans, or financial obligations you have. Next, review your income and expenses. Track all sources of income, whether it's your salary, child support, or any side earnings. Compare this with your monthly expenses, including rent, utilities, groceries, and other bills. Identifying financial dependencies on the narcissist is also essential. Determine if there are any joint accounts, shared debts, or financial commitments that tie you to them. Understanding these dependencies helps you plan your next steps more effectively.

Creating a financial plan is the next step toward achieving financial independence. Begin by setting short-term and long-term financial goals. Short-term goals might include:

- Paying off a small debt.

- Saving for an emergency fund.

- Reducing monthly expenses.

Long-term goals could be buying a home, investing for retirement, or funding your children's education. Once you've set your goals, create a budget to track your spending. List your income and categorize your expenses. Identify areas where you can cut back and allocate more towards savings and debt repayment. Building an emergency fund is crucial. Three to six months' worth of living expenses is what you should aim to save. This fund will act as a financial cushion in case of unexpected events, providing you with peace of mind and security.

Securing financial resources during the transition can alleviate some of the financial strain. Apply for financial assistance programs offered by government and non-profit organizations. These programs can provide temporary relief and support as you work towards financial independence. Seeking temporary financial support from friends or family is another option. Don't hesitate to contact trusted individuals who can assist during this challenging time. Exploring options for spousal or child support is also vital. Legal avenues exist to ensure you receive the financial support you are entitled to. Consulting with a lawyer can help you navigate these options and secure the necessary support.

Building financial literacy is an ongoing process that empowers you to manage your finances better. Taking financial education courses can provide you with valuable knowledge and skills. Many community centers, non-profits, and online platforms offer budgeting, investing, and debt management courses. Reading books or online resources on personal finance is another excellent way to improve your financial literacy. Numerous books and websites are dedicated to helping individuals understand and manage their finances effectively. Consulting with a financial advisor can provide personalized guidance and strategies tailored to your situation. A financial advisor can help you create a comprehensive financial plan, invest wisely, and achieve your long-term financial goals.

By taking control of your finances, creating a detailed plan, securing resources, and building your financial literacy, you lay a strong foundation for independence and stability. The journey towards financial independence is empowering, providing you with the tools and confidence needed to rebuild your life. As you move forward, remember that each step you take brings you closer to a secure and fulfilling future.

In the following chapter, we will explore the role of therapy and professional help in your recovery journey, providing insights and strategies to support your mental and emotional well-being.

Chapter 8: The Role of Therapy and Professional Help

Imagine feeling like you're trapped in a maze, each turn leading you further into confusion and pain. That's what surviving narcissistic abuse can feel like. Therapy can be the guiding light that helps you navigate this maze, leading you toward clarity and healing. The right therapist can provide the support and tools necessary to rebuild your life. But finding that therapist can seem daunting. This chapter will guide you through the process of finding a specialized therapist who understands the complexities of narcissistic abuse.

8.1 Finding the Right Therapist

Finding a therapist with specialized knowledge in narcissistic personality disorder (NPD) is crucial. Narcissistic abuse involves intricate emotional manipulation and trauma, which requires a therapist who understands these complexities. They need to be well-versed in the tactics of gaslighting, love bombing, and hoovering and how these behaviours impact your mental health. A therapist experienced in NPD will know how to navigate these challenges and provide effective treatment.

Researching potential therapists is the first step in this journey. Start by looking for therapists with relevant credentials and experience. Certifications in trauma therapy, cognitive-behavioural therapy (CBT), or eye movement desensitization and reprocessing (EMDR) are good indicators of their expertise. Reading reviews and testimonials from other clients can provide insights into their effectiveness and approach. Asking for referrals from trusted sources, such as friends, family, or support groups, can also point you in the right direction. Personal recommendations often come with firsthand accounts of a therapist's methods and demeanour.

Once you have a list of potential therapists, the next step is to conduct initial consultations to determine if they are the right fit. Prepare a list of questions to ask during these consultations. Inquire about their experience with narcissistic abuse, their therapeutic approach, and their familiarity with NPD. Assess their communication style and empathy. Do they listen actively? Do they show understanding and validation of your experiences? Comfort and rapport are essential. You need to feel safe and understood in their presence. If you feel discomfort or sense they are not fully grasping your situation, it might be best to continue your search.

Recognizing red flags in therapists is equally important. A lack of understanding or minimizing the impact of narcissistic abuse is a significant warning sign. If a therapist downplays your experiences or suggests that you are overreacting, they are not the right fit for you. Inadequate experience with trauma or abuse survivors can also be a red flag. Therapists lacking this experience may not have the tools or insights to help you navigate your healing process effectively. Unprofessional behaviour or boundary violations are serious concerns. Trust your instincts. If something feels off, it's okay to seek another therapist.

Interactive Element: Therapist Evaluation Checklist

Use this checklist during your consultations to evaluate potential therapists:

- *Experience with Narcissistic Abuse*: Do they have a background in dealing with NPD and emotional manipulation?

- *Therapeutic Approach*: Are they familiar with therapies like CBT or EMDR that are effective for trauma?

- *Communication Style*: Do they listen actively and validate your experiences?

- *Comfort and Rapport*: Do you feel safe and understood in their presence?

- *Red Flags*: Do they minimize your experiences or exhibit unprofessional behaviour?

Finding the right therapist takes time and patience, but it's a crucial step in your healing journey. You deserve a therapist who understands the depth of your pain and can guide you toward recovery. This process is about finding someone who can walk with you through the maze, offering support and tools to help you navigate each twist and turn.

Remember, switching therapists is okay if the current one isn't a good fit. Your healing is the priority. Don't settle for anything less than a therapist who makes you feel seen, heard, and understood. Trust and rapport are foundational to effective therapy. Consider their style, experience, and how they make you feel. The right therapist will help you stabilize your nervous system and empower you to rebuild your life with self-love and self-empowerment.

8.2 Types of Therapy for Narcissistic Abuse Survivors

Imagine you've been walking through a dark forest, stumbling over roots and branches, unsure of which path to take. Therapy can be the flashlight guiding you through this darkness. Various therapeutic approaches can help you process the trauma of narcissistic abuse and rebuild your life.

Cognitive Behavioral Therapy (CBT) is one of the most effective treatments for survivors of narcissistic abuse. This type of therapy focuses on identifying and challenging cognitive distortions—those negative thought patterns that have been ingrained in you through years of manipulation. For example, you might believe, "I'm not good enough" or "Everything is my fault." CBT helps you recognize these distortions and reframe them into healthier thought patterns. Instead of thinking, "I can't do anything right," you learn to think, "I am capable and deserving of success." This shift in thinking leads to practicing new coping strategies, such as assertiveness and self-compassion. Over time, these new habits replace the old, destructive ones, helping you regain control over your thoughts and emotions.

Eye Movement Desensitization and Reprocessing (EMDR) is another powerful therapy for trauma survivors. EMDR uses bilateral stimulation, such as eye movements or tapping, to help you reprocess traumatic memories. Imagine your mind as a cluttered attic; EMDR helps you sort through the clutter, reducing the emotional intensity of those painful memories. This therapy enhances overall emotional regulation, allowing you to respond to triggers with more stability. During an EMDR session, you might recall a traumatic event while following the therapist's finger movements with your eyes. This process helps your brain reframe the memory, making it less distressing. The result is a significant reduction in PTSD symptoms and an increased sense of emotional well-being.

Schema Therapy goes a step further by addressing deep-seated patterns and beliefs formed during childhood. These maladaptive schemas are like blueprints for how you see the world and yourself. For example, if you grew up in an environment where you were constantly criticized, you might develop a schema of "defectiveness" or "unworthiness." Schema Therapy helps you identify these harmful schemas and work on changing them. This involves challenging the long-standing negative patterns and building healthier coping mechanisms. Through techniques like imagery re-scripting and cognitive restructuring, you learn to see yourself in a more positive light. This therapy not only helps you heal from past abuse but also equips you with tools to build healthier relationships moving forward.

Dialectical Behavior Therapy (DBT) offers a comprehensive approach to emotional regulation and relationship skills. DBT was initially developed for borderline personality disorder and has proven effective for many forms of emotional dysregulation, including those resulting from narcissistic abuse. One of the core components of DBT is mindfulness. Mindfulness teaches you to stay present and fully engage with your current experience rather than being overwhelmed by past traumas or future anxieties. DBT also teaches emotion regulation techniques, helping you manage intense emotions without resorting to destructive behaviours. Skills like distress tolerance and interpersonal effectiveness are crucial for maintaining healthy relationships. For instance, you might learn how to communicate your needs assertively without escalating conflicts.

Each of these therapies offers unique benefits and can be tailored to your specific needs. CBT helps you reframe negative thoughts and develop healthier coping strategies. EMDR allows you to process and resolve trauma, reducing its emotional intensity. Schema Therapy targets deep-rooted beliefs and patterns, helping you build a more positive self-image. DBT equips you with skills for emotional regulation and effective communication. These therapies can be used individually or in combination, depending on what works best for you.

Finding the right therapeutic approach is a personal journey. What works for one person might not work for another, and that's okay. The key is to stay open to trying different methods and finding what resonates with you. Therapy is not a one-size-fits-all solution; it's a tailored experience designed to meet your unique needs. Whether you resonate more with the cognitive restructuring of CBT, the trauma processing of EMDR, the deep exploration of Schema Therapy, or the skill-building focus of DBT, the goal remains the same: to help you heal and reclaim your life.

8.3 The Benefits of Support Groups

Support groups can be a lifeline for survivors of narcissistic abuse. Finding a community that understands your experience can provide immense relief when you've been isolated and manipulated. These groups offer a haven where shared experiences and empathy create an environment of understanding and validation. In a support group, you'll find others who have walked a similar path, and this connection can reduce feelings of isolation. Knowing that you're not alone in your struggle can be incredibly comforting. The empathy you receive from peers who genuinely understand your pain fosters a sense of belonging and support. This peer support becomes a source of encouragement, helping you navigate the complexities of recovery.

There are different types of support groups available to survivors, each offering unique benefits.

- In-person support groups provide face-to-face interactions that can be deeply reassuring. These groups often meet regularly in community centers, hospitals, or therapy offices. The physical presence of others can make the experience more intimate and supportive.

- Online forums and communities, on the other hand, offer the flexibility of connecting from anywhere. These platforms allow you to share your story and receive support anytime, making them accessible for those with busy schedules or limited mobility.

- Facilitated groups led by professionals can provide a structured environment where a trained therapist guides the discussions. These groups often incorporate therapeutic techniques and provide a safe space for deeper emotional exploration.

Finding the right support group requires a bit of research and discernment. Start by looking into local options through community centers, hospitals, or mental health organizations. Online searches can also yield a plethora of virtual communities and forums dedicated to survivors of narcissistic abuse. Evaluate the focus and structure of each group. Some might be more general, while others cater to specific experiences, such as co-parenting with a narcissist or healing from childhood narcissistic abuse.

Attend a few sessions to get a feel for the group's dynamics. Notice how the group members interact, the facilitator's approach, and whether you feel comfortable and supported. It's okay to try out several groups before finding one that resonates with you.

Maximizing the benefits of support groups involves active participation and setting personal goals. Engage in the discussions and share your experiences openly. The more you put into the group, the more you'll get out of it. Listening to others can provide new perspectives and insights that you might not have considered. Setting personal goals for your participation can also be helpful. For example, you might aim to share at least once per session or to reach out to another group member for support outside of meetings. Utilize the resources and recommendations provided by the group. Many support groups offer additional tools, such as reading materials, coping strategies, and referrals to other helpful services.

Support groups can provide a sense of community and validation that is often missing in the lives of survivors. The shared experiences and empathy found in these groups reduce feelings of isolation and offer peer support and encouragement. Whether you choose an in-person group, an online community, or a facilitated group led by a professional, the key is to find a space where you feel understood and supported. Engage actively, set personal goals, and make the most of the resources available to you. This communal support can be a powerful complement to individual therapy, offering another layer of healing and empowerment.

8.4 Complementing Therapy with Self-Help

Combining professional therapy with self-help strategies can significantly enhance your healing process. While therapy provides a structured environment and expert guidance, self-help empowers you to take an active role in your recovery. This dual approach can accelerate your progress, offering a sense of control and fostering personal growth. Self-help tools and resources act as additional coping mechanisms, filling in the gaps between therapy sessions and providing continuous support. They equip you with practical skills and knowledge, making the therapeutic process more effective and helping you build a robust foundation for long-term well-being.

Self-help books like this one and resources specifically designed for survivors of narcissistic abuse can be invaluable. They can be powerful companions on your path to recovery, offering wisdom and encouragement when you need it most.

Developing a personalized self-care routine is crucial for supporting your healing journey. Start by incorporating mindfulness and relaxation techniques into your daily life. Deep breathing, meditation, and progressive muscle relaxation can help calm your mind and reduce stress. Apps like *Headspace* and *Calm* offer a variety of guided meditations and mindfulness exercises that are easy to follow and can be done anywhere to help you manage stress and stay grounded. Utilizing online tools and apps can complement your therapy and self-help efforts. These apps provide tools for relaxation, sleep improvement, and even quick exercises for moments of anxiety. Journaling and mood-tracking apps, like *Daylio* or *Penzu*, can help you monitor your emotional state and identify patterns in your mood and behaviour. Writing down your thoughts and feelings can be therapeutic, helping you process your experiences and gain insights into your emotional triggers. Online therapy platforms, such as *BetterHelp* or *Talkspace*, can offer additional support, providing access to professional therapists through text, video, or phone sessions. These platforms can be especially useful if you need extra guidance between in-person therapy appointments.

Engaging in physical activities and hobbies is another vital component of self-care. Exercise releases endorphins, which can improve your mood and energy levels. Whether it's yoga, dancing, or simply walking in nature, find activities that bring you joy and relaxation. Hobbies like painting, gardening, or reading can also provide a creative outlet and a sense of accomplishment. Prioritizing rest and nutrition is equally important. Ensure you get enough sleep, eat balanced meals, and stay hydrated. A well-nourished body supports a healthy mind, making coping with stress and emotional challenges easier.

Combining professional therapy with self-help strategies allows you to take an active role in your healing process. This approach enhances the therapeutic experience, empowering you to make continuous progress and build a strong foundation for long-term well-being. Self-help books and resources offer valuable insights and practical advice. At the same time, a personalized self-care routine supports your emotional and physical health. Utilizing online tools and apps provides additional coping mechanisms and continuous support. Together, these strategies create a comprehensive support system that fosters healing and personal growth.

Chapter 9: Mindfulness and Holistic Healing

Imagine standing in the middle of a serene forest, the air crisp and fresh, the sounds of rustling leaves and chirping birds surrounding you. For a moment, you feel completely present, your worries melting away. This is the essence of mindfulness—being fully engaged in the present moment. Mindfulness can be a powerful tool for healing, especially for survivors of narcissistic abuse. It helps you regain emotional balance, reduce stress, and improve emotional regulation.

9.1 Mindfulness Techniques for Emotional Balance

Mindfulness plays a crucial role in healing from narcissistic abuse by increasing self-awareness, reducing stress, and enhancing emotional regulation. When you practice mindfulness, you become more attuned to your thoughts, emotions, and physical sensations. This heightened awareness allows you to recognize and address emotional triggers before they spiral out of control. For survivors, this means breaking free from the constant state of hypervigilance and fear and, instead, finding moments of peace and clarity.

One of the most immediate benefits of mindfulness is the reduction of stress and anxiety. Narcissistic abuse often leaves you in a perpetual state of tension, always anticipating the next conflict or manipulation. Mindfulness techniques like breath awareness and body scans help calm the nervous system. By focusing on your breath or scanning your body for tension, you can shift your attention away from stressors and bring yourself back to a state of calm. This practice reduces immediate anxiety and builds resilience over time, making it easier to handle stressful situations.

Another significant benefit of mindfulness is improved emotional regulation. Emotional regulation refers to the ability to manage and respond to your emotions in a healthy way. For survivors, this can be particularly challenging, as the emotional rollercoaster of abuse often leaves you feeling out of control. Mindfulness helps you observe your emotions without judgment, allowing you to process them more effectively. This means you can respond to triggers with greater clarity and calm rather than reacting impulsively.

To start incorporating mindfulness into your life, consider these basic practices. Breath awareness exercises are a simple yet powerful way to center yourself. Find a quiet place, sit comfortably, and focus on your breath. Notice the sensation of the air entering and leaving your nostrils. If your mind wanders, gently bring your focus back to your breath. This practice helps anchor you in the present moment and can be done anywhere, at any t ime.

Body scan meditations are another effective technique. Lie down or sit comfortably, close your eyes, and slowly scan your body from head to toe. Pay attention to any areas of tension or discomfort, and consciously relax those muscles. This practice helps you reconnect with your physical sensations, promoting a sense of grounding and relaxation. It's particularly helpful for those who feel disconnected from their bodies due to the trauma of abuse. Combining movement with mindfulness is a practice called mindful walking. Firstly, find a quiet place to walk, such as a park or a quiet street. As you walk, focus on the sensation of the movement of your legs, your feet touching the ground, and the rhythm of your breath. Notice the sights, sounds, and smells around you. This practice brings you into the present moment. It provides the added benefit of physical exercise, which can further reduce stress and improve mood.

Incorporating mindfulness into your daily routine doesn't have to be complicated. Start by setting aside specific times for mindfulness practice. This could be as little as five minutes in the morning or before bed. As you become more comfortable with the practice, gradually increase the duration. You can also infuse mindfulness into everyday activities, such as eating or commuting. For example, pay attention to your food's taste, texture, and smell while eating. While commuting, focus on the sights and sounds around you rather than letting your mind wander.

Creating a calming environment for mindfulness practice can enhance its benefits. Choose a quiet space where you won't be disturbed, and consider adding elements that promote relaxation, such as soft lighting, calming music, or essential oils. This environment can become a sanctuary where you can retreat whenever you need to center yourself.

Real-life examples illustrate the transformative power of mindfulness. Take Sarah, a survivor of narcissistic abuse who struggled with anxiety and panic attacks. She began practicing breath awareness exercises, focusing on her breath whenever she felt anxious. Over time, she found that these exercises helped her manage her anxiety more effectively, allowing her to regain control over her emotions. Another example is John, who felt disconnected from his body after years of emotional manipulation. He started doing body scan meditations, which helped him reconnect with his physical sensations and reduce tension. These practices became a cornerstone of his healing journey, providing him with tools to navigate the challenges he faced.

Mindfulness offers a pathway to emotional balance and resilience for survivors of narcissistic abuse. By increasing self-awareness, reducing stress, and improving emotional regulation, mindfulness helps you reclaim control over your emotions and find moments of peace amidst the chaos. Whether through breath awareness, body scans, or mindful walking, these simple practices can profoundly impact your well-being.

9.2 Meditation Practices for Healing

Meditation can be a lifeline for survivors of narcissistic abuse. It offers a way to sift through the emotional debris and find a deeper sense of peace. One of the most compelling benefits of meditation is enhanced emotional clarity. After enduring manipulation and gaslighting, your sense of reality can feel distorted. Meditation helps clear the fog, allowing you to reconnect with your genuine emotions and thoughts. It acts like a mental detox, flushing out the negativity that has clouded your judgment and self-perception.

Meditation is also instrumental in reducing symptoms of PTSD and anxiety, common afflictions for survivors. The act of sitting quietly and focusing inward can help calm an overactive mind. It decreases your body's stress hormones, allowing you to move from a fight-or-flight state to one of rest and relaxation. Studies have shown that regular meditation can significantly lower anxiety levels and improve mood, providing a natural antidote to the emotional upheaval caused by abuse. The sense of inner peace that meditation fosters can't be overstated. It creates a sanctuary within yourself, a refuge you can retreat to whenever the outside world feels overwhelming.

There are several types of meditation, each offering unique benefits:

- *Guided meditation* is a fantastic starting point for beginners. In this practice, a guide leads you through a series of visualizations and breathing exercises, helping you to focus and relax. This can be particularly helpful if your mind tends to wander or you find it difficult to concentrate.

- *Loving-kindness meditation, or Metta,* involves directing love and compassion towards yourself and others. This practice can be incredibly healing, helping to rebuild your self-esteem and foster positive emotions.

- *Visualization meditation* involves imagining a peaceful scene or a positive outcome. It can help lift one's spirits and provide a mental escape from daily stressors.

Starting a meditation practice may seem daunting, but it's simpler than you think. Begin by choosing a comfortable, quiet space where you won't be disturbed. This could be a corner of your bedroom, a spot in the garden, or even your car during a lunch break. Setting the right environment is crucial for a successful meditation session. Next, set a timer to help you stay focused. Start with just five minutes and gradually increase the duration as you become more comfortable. Focus on your breath or a specific mantra. This could be a word or phrase that brings you comfort, like "peace" or "I am safe." The key is to keep your mind engaged and prevent it from wandering.

Resources for guided meditations are plentiful and can make the process even more accessible. Online platforms like *Insight Timer* and *Calm* offer a wide range of guided meditations tailored to different needs, including anxiety relief, emotional healing, and self-love. These platforms often feature meditations led by experienced teachers, providing you with professional guidance at your fingertips. Meditation apps are another excellent resource. Apps like *Headspace* and *Simple Habit* offer specific programs designed to help you navigate the complexities of healing from trauma. Books and audio recordings from renowned meditation teachers can also provide valuable insights and techniques. Titles like "The Miracle of Mindfulness" by Thich Nhat Hanh or "Wherever You Go, There You Are" by Jon Kabat-Zinn are excellent starting points.

Meditation offers a pathway to emotional clarity, reduced anxiety, and a greater sense of inner peace. By exploring different types of meditation and incorporating them into your daily routine, you can create a powerful toolkit for healing. Whether you choose guided meditation, loving-kindness meditation, or visualization, each practice brings unique benefits that can help you reclaim your emotional well-being. Start small, use available resources, and gradually build a practice that supports your journey towards healing.

9.3 The Role of Somatic Therapies

Survivors of narcissistic abuse often carry the weight of their trauma not just in their minds but also in their bodies. Somatic therapies focus on this intricate connection between body and mind, offering a pathway to healing that integrates both. Trauma can become "trapped" in the body, manifesting as muscle tension, chronic pain, or even disrupted sleep. Somatic therapies aim to release this stored trauma, providing relief from physical symptoms and fostering a sense of safety within one's own body. By enhancing bodily awareness, these therapies help you become more attuned to your physical sensations and emotions, enabling better self-regulation and emotional balance.

One prominent type of somatic therapy is **Somatic Experiencing (SE)**. Developed by Dr. Peter Levine, SE focuses on releasing the trauma stored in the nervous system. It involves gently guiding you to revisit traumatic experiences in a safe and controlled manner, allowing your body to complete the natural fight, flight or freeze responses that were interrupted during the traumatic event. This process helps discharge the pent-up energy associated with trauma, reducing symptoms of anxiety and PTSD. SE practitioners often use techniques like grounding and centring to help you stay present and connected to your body during the sessions.

Sensorimotor Psychotherapy is another effective modality. It integrates cognitive and somatic approaches to address the effects of trauma. This therapy emphasizes exploring how trauma impacts your body and behaviours. Through mindful body awareness and movement, Sensorimotor Psychotherapy helps you process traumatic memories and develop healthier coping mechanisms. The focus is on creating a safe space where you can explore and release the physical sensations associated with trauma, allowing for a more holistic healing experience.

Bioenergetic Analysis is a third modality that combines psychotherapy with physical exercises to release emotional tension. Developed by Dr. Alexander Lowen, this approach emphasizes understanding how emotional conflicts manifest in the body. Bioenergetic exercises, such as grounding and expressive movements, help release physical tension and restore the natural flow of energy in the body. This therapy aims to reconnect you with your physical sensations, promoting a sense of vitality and emotional well-being.

You can also practice simple somatic exercises on your own to support your healing. Grounding exercises can help you reconnect with your body and the present moment. One such exercise involves standing with your feet firmly planted on the ground, feeling the earth beneath you. Focus on the sensations in your feet and legs, allowing yourself to feel supported and grounded. This practice can be particularly helpful during moments of stress or anxiety, providing a sense of stability and calm.

Movement and shaking practices are effective for releasing physical tension and stored trauma. Find a quiet space where you can move freely. Start by gently shaking your arms, legs, and torso, allowing any tension to release. Gradually increase the intensity of the shaking, letting your body move in whatever way feels natural. This practice helps discharge pent-up energy and emotions, which leaves you feeling more relaxed and centered.

Breathwork is another powerful tool for calming the nervous system. Begin by finding a comfortable seated position. Close your eyes and take a deep breath in through your nose, allowing your belly to expand. Hold the breath for a few seconds, then exhale slowly through your mouth, releasing any tension. Repeat this process several times, focusing on the rhythm of your breath. This practice helps activate the parasympathetic nervous system, promoting relaxation and reducing stress.

Finding a qualified somatic therapist can enhance your healing journey. Start by researching therapists with specialized training in somatic modalities. Look for certifications from reputable organizations and check their experience in working with trauma survivors. Initial consultations are crucial for assessing fit and comfort. Discuss your goals and concerns during these sessions, and observe how the therapist interacts with you. A good therapist will create a safe and supportive environment, making you feel heard and understood.

Somatic therapies offer a holistic approach to healing that recognizes the profound connection between body and mind. By releasing stored trauma, enhancing bodily awareness, and promoting self-regulation, these therapies can provide significant relief from the physical and emotional symptoms of trauma. Whether through professional guidance or simple exercises you can practice at home, somatic therapies open new pathways for healing and reclaiming your sense of self.

9.4 Integrating Yoga and Physical Wellness

Yoga offers a holistic approach to healing that addresses the physical, emotional, and mental aspects of well-being. For survivors of narcissistic abuse, yoga can be particularly beneficial. One of its key advantages is enhancing body awareness and flexibility. The gentle movements and stretches help you reconnect with your body, which may have felt foreign or disconnected due to trauma. Regular practice can also improve flexibility, making everyday activities easier and more comfortable. This physical engagement promotes a sense of strength and control over your body, which is empowering after enduring manipulation and control.

Other significant benefits of yoga include reducing stress and promoting relaxation. The practice encourages deep, mindful breathing and focused movement, which activate the parasympathetic nervous system. This helps counteract the stress response, lowering levels of cortisol, the body's primary stress hormone. As you move through the poses, you find moments of stillness and peace, allowing your mind to relax and your body to release tension. This reduction in stress can improve sleep, enhance mood, and increase overall well-being.

Building inner strength and resilience is another powerful outcome of a consistent yoga practice. Yoga challenges you to stay present and push through physical and mental discomfort. As you progress, you build resilience, not just in your muscles but in your mind. This inner strength translates into greater emotional resilience, helping you navigate the ups and downs of recovery with more stability and confidence.

Several styles of yoga are particularly beneficial for trauma recovery:

Trauma-sensitive yoga is specifically designed to create a safe and supportive environment. It focuses on gentle, mindful movements and emphasizes choice and agency. This approach helps you feel more in control of your body and your practice, which is crucial for those who have experienced trauma.

Restorative yoga is another excellent option. It involves holding gentle poses for extended periods, often with the support of props like blankets and bolsters. This practice promotes deep relaxation and helps release physical and emotional tension.

Hatha yoga, which includes a mix of postures, breathing exercises, and meditation, is also beneficial. It provides a balanced approach, combining physical activity with mental focus and relaxation.

Creating a personalized yoga routine can make your practice more effective and enjoyable. Start by choosing appropriate poses and sequences that meet your needs and comfort level. If you're new to yoga, consider starting with simple poses like *Child's Pose, Cat-Cow, and Downward Dog*. These poses are gentle yet effective in promoting flexibility and relaxation. As you become more comfortable, you can gradually incorporate more challenging poses. Setting up a dedicated practice space can enhance your experience. Choose a quiet, comfortable area where you can practice without distractions. Consider adding elements that promote relaxation, such as soft lighting, calming music, or essential oils.

Incorporating breathwork and meditation into your routine can deepen its benefits. Start each session with a few minutes of focused breathing to center yourself. You can use techniques like diaphragmatic breathing, where you inhale deeply into your belly, or alternate nostril breathing, which helps balance the nervous system. End your practice with a short meditation to calm your mind and integrate the benefits of your physical practice. This combination of movement, breathwork, and meditation creates a holistic practice that nurtures both body and mind.

There are numerous resources available to support your yoga journey. Online yoga classes and platforms, such as *Yoga with Adriene*, offer a wide range of classes tailored to different needs and levels. These platforms often include classes specifically designed for trauma recovery, providing guided support from experienced instructors. Yoga studios that offer trauma-sensitive classes are another valuable resource. These studios create a safe and supportive environment where you can practice with others who understand your experiences. Books and DVDs from experienced yoga instructors can also provide valuable guidance and inspiration. Titles like "The Healing Power of Yoga" by Dr. Timothy McCall or "Yoga for Emotional Balance" by Bo Forbes offer insights and techniques to enhance your practice.

Integrating yoga and physical wellness into your recovery process offers a holistic approach to healing that addresses the physical, emotional, and mental aspects of well-being. By enhancing body awareness, reducing stress, and building inner strength, yoga provides a pathway to reclaiming your sense of self and finding peace and resilience amidst the challenges of recovery. Whether through trauma-sensitive yoga, restorative yoga, or Hatha yoga, each practice offers unique benefits that can support you on your journey towards healing and empowerment.

As we move forward, we will delve into the challenges and strategies for co-parenting with a narcissist. This topic presents unique difficulties and requires careful navigation. Understanding these dynamics and learning effective strategies will help you protect yourself and your children while fostering a healthier and more stable environment.

Chapter 10: Parenting and Protecting Children

Imagine watching your child play happily one moment, only to see them withdraw into a shell of anxiety and sadness the next. This drastic shift can be a stark indicator of the emotional turmoil they're experiencing. As a parent, it's heartbreaking to witness these changes, especially when they stem from the manipulative behaviour of a narcissistic co-parent. Recognizing the signs of emotional distress in your children is the first step in helping them navigate the complex world of narcissistic abuse.

10.1 Recognizing the Impact on Children

Children are incredibly perceptive and often internalize the conflict and tension around them. Increased anxiety or depression can manifest in various ways. You might notice your child becoming more irritable or withdrawn, losing interest in activities they once enjoyed, or expressing constant worry. Behavioural problems at school are also common. These might include sudden drops in academic performance, frequent outbursts, or difficulty concentrating. Teachers might report that your child is acting out or becoming increasingly isolated.

Withdrawal from friends and activities is another red flag. A once social and active child might suddenly prefer to stay home, avoiding interactions and group activities. They might make excuses to skip playdates or extracurricular activities, choosing solitude over socialization. Frequent nightmares or sleep disturbances are also telltale signs. Your child might wake up crying, have trouble falling asleep, or experience restless nights filled with anxiety. These sleep issues can exacerbate their emotional distress, leading to a vicious cycle of fatigue and heightened anxiety.

The long-term effects of narcissistic abuse on children can be profound. They might develop low self-esteem, constantly doubting their worth and abilities. This lack of self-confidence can follow them into adulthood, affecting their personal and professional relationships. Difficulty forming healthy relationships is another significant impact. Children of narcissistic parents often struggle to trust others, fearing manipulation and betrayal. This fear can lead to emotional distance, making it hard for them to form deep, meaningful connections.

Increased risk of mental health issues is a serious concern. Exposure to narcissistic abuse can make children more susceptible to conditions like anxiety, depression, and PTSD. These mental health challenges can persist into adulthood, affecting their overall quality of life. Understanding these long-term effects is crucial for providing the support and intervention your child needs to heal and thrive.

Narcissistic parents often use manipulative tactics to control or alienate children from the other parent. One common method is using children as pawns in conflicts. They might make the child feel guilty for spending time with the other parent or use them to relay hurtful messages. This places the child in an unfair and stressful position, forcing them to navigate adult conflicts. Gaslighting and invalidating children's feelings is another tactic. The narcissistic parent might dismiss the child's emotions, telling them they're overreacting or imagining problems. This invalidation can make children doubt their feelings and perceptions, leading to confusion and self-doubt.

Creating loyalty conflicts is a particularly damaging tactic. The narcissistic parent might try to turn the child against the other parent, creating a divide that forces the child to choose sides. This can strain the child's relationship with both parents, fostering feelings of guilt and divided loyalty. Recognizing these manipulative tactics is essential for protecting your child and providing the emotional support they need.

Consider the story of Emily, a bright and bubbly eight-year-old who suddenly became withdrawn and anxious. Her father, a narcissist, frequently used her as a pawn to hurt her mother. He would make Emily feel guilty for enjoying time with her mother, telling her that she was betraying him. This constant conflict and emotional manipulation took a toll on Emily, leading to increased anxiety and frequent nightmares. Her mother noticed these changes and sought professional help, providing Emily with the support and validation she needed to understand that her feelings were valid and that the conflict was not her fault.

Then there's Jake, a teenager who struggled with self-esteem issues after years of being belittled by his narcissistic parent. His mother constantly compared him to others, telling him he would never be good enough. This relentless criticism eroded Jake's self-worth, making him doubt his abilities and value. With the support of his father and a therapist, Jake began to rebuild his self-esteem, learning to recognize his strengths and achievements.

Interactive Element: Emotional Distress Checklist

Use this checklist to identify signs of emotional distress in your child:

- Increased anxiety or depression
- Behavioural problems at school
- Withdrawal from friends and activities
- Frequent nightmares or sleep disturbances

If you notice several of these signs, it may be time to seek professional help for your child. Addressing these issues early can significantly improve their emotional well-being and development.

Recognizing the impact of narcissistic abuse on children is the first step in helping them heal. By understanding the signs of emotional distress, the long-term effects, and the manipulative tactics used by narcissists, you can provide the support and intervention your child needs to thrive.

10.2 Building Resilience in Your Children

Creating a supportive and loving environment is the cornerstone of building resilience in your children. Providing consistent love and attention makes them feel valued and secure. This sense of security is crucial, especially when they're dealing with the emotional upheaval caused by a narcissistic parent. Establishing predictable routines can also be incredibly grounding for children. Knowing what to expect each day helps them feel more in control, reducing anxiety and fostering a sense of stability. Encouraging open communication is equally important. Let your children know that they can talk to you about anything and be there to listen without judgment. This openness builds trust and lets them know they are not alone in navigating their feelings.

Helping your children develop emotional intelligence can equip them with the skills needed to manage their emotions and cope with stress. Start by teaching them to recognize and name their emotions. Simple exercises like asking them to describe how they feel and why can be very effective. Practicing empathy and understanding is another key component. Encourage them to consider how others might feel in different situations, fostering a sense of compassion and emotional awareness. Managing stress and difficult emotions is a skill that will serve them throughout their lives. Teach them techniques like deep breathing, mindfulness, or even simple counting exercises to calm their minds when they feel overwhelmed.

Healthy self-expression is vital for your children's emotional well-being. Support them in finding constructive ways to express their thoughts and feelings. Creative outlets like art or writing can be incredibly therapeutic. Give them materials to draw, paint, or write about their experiences and emotions. Verbal expression through open conversations is also crucial. Make it a point to regularly sit down and talk with your children about their day, feelings, and any concerns they might have. Physical activities like sports or dance can also be an excellent way for them to release pent-up energy and emotions. Encourage them to participate in activities they enjoy and that allow them to express themselves physically.

Promoting positive self-esteem is another critical aspect of building resilience. Praise your children's efforts and accomplishments, no matter how small. This recognition helps them feel proud of themselves and builds their confidence. Setting realistic and achievable goals can also boost their self-esteem. Help them set small, manageable goals and celebrate their achievements along the way. Encourage self-compassion and self-care by teaching them to be kind to themselves. Remind them that it's okay to make mistakes and that they should treat themselves with the same kindness they would offer a friend.

Imagine a young girl named Lily who loves to draw. Her mother provides her with various art supplies and encourages her to express her feelings through her drawings. Lily finds solace in her art, creating vibrant pieces that reflect her inner world. Her mother regularly praises her for her creativity and effort, helping Lily build a strong sense of self-worth. Lily also learns to talk about her feelings during their evening chats, where her mother listens and validates her emotions. This supportive environment helps Lily develop resilience, enabling her to cope with the challenges posed by her narcissistic father.

In another scenario, a boy named Max struggles with anxiety due to the unpredictable behaviour of his narcissistic parent. His mother introduces him to mindfulness exercises, teaching him to focus on his breath and stay present. Max practices these exercises daily, finding that they help him manage his anxiety. His mother also encourages him to participate in a local soccer team, where he channels his energy and builds friendships. His mother's consistent praise and support, combined with the skills he learns through mindfulness and sports, help Max develop resilience and a positive self-image.

These strategies—providing consistent love and attention, establishing predictable routines, encouraging open communication, teaching emotional intelligence, supporting healthy self-expression, and promoting positive self-esteem—are powerful tools for building resilience in your children. By implementing these practices, you can help them navigate the challenges they face and emerge stronger and more confident.

10.3 Co-Parenting Strategies with a Narcissist

Establishing clear boundaries and expectations with a narcissistic co-parent is crucial for maintaining your sanity and protecting your children. Defining acceptable behaviour during interactions is the first step. Set firm guidelines on what is and isn't acceptable. For instance, make it clear that personal attacks or derogatory comments are off-limits. Use written communication to document agreements. This could be through emails or co-parenting apps. Written records serve as a reference and can be invaluable if disputes arise. Setting limits on discussions about personal matters is also essential. Keep conversations focused solely on the children. Avoid diving into personal issues or rehashing past conflicts. This helps maintain a professional tone and prevents the narcissist from using personal information against you.

Maintaining a business-like relationship with your narcissistic co-parent can be a game-changer. Treat your interactions as if you're dealing with a colleague. This mindset helps you keep emotions in check and focus on what matters—your children's well-being. Avoid emotional triggers and conflicts by sticking to factual, child-focused communication. For example, instead of saying, "You never pick up the kids on time," say, "The kids need to be picked up at 3 PM." This approach minimizes the chance of arguments and keeps the conversation productive. Use a neutral tone and language. Avoid letting frustration or anger seep into your words.

Remaining calm and composed can defuse potential conflicts and set a positive example for your children.

Using parenting apps and tools can streamline communication and reduce misunderstandings. Co-parenting apps like *OurFamilyWizard* or *TalkingParents* are specifically designed to facilitate organized and documented communication. These apps offer features like shared calendars, task lists, and expense tracking, making it easier to manage parenting schedules and responsibilities. Shared calendars ensure both parents are on the same page regarding custody arrangements and important events. Task lists can help keep track of responsibilities, such as school projects or medical appointments. Online platforms for tracking expenses and agreements provide transparency and accountability, reducing the chance of disputes over financial matters.

Planning for conflict resolution is another vital aspect of co-parenting with a narcissist. Conflicts are inevitable, but how you handle them can make a significant difference. Seeking mediation or professional help when necessary can provide an objective perspective and facilitate fair resolutions. A trained mediator can help both parties communicate more effectively and find common ground. Establishing a conflict resolution protocol can also be beneficial. This could involve setting specific steps to follow when a disagreement arises, such as taking a time-out to cool down and then discussing the issue calmly. Prioritizing the children's well-being in all decisions is paramount. Always ask yourself, "What is best for the children?" before making decisions. This focus helps keep the conversation on track and ensures that your children's needs are at the forefront.

Imagine a scenario where you and your narcissistic co-parent disagree on a school event. Instead of letting the conversation spiral into a heated argument, you refer to your written communication. "According to our calendar on OurFamilyWizard, you agreed to take the kids to the event this Saturday," you calmly state. If the disagreement persists, you suggest mediation. "I think we should involve a mediator to find a fair solution," you propose. Keeping the communication factual and focused on the children avoids unnecessary conflict and sets a positive example for your kids.

Another example is discussing financial responsibilities. Instead of arguing about expenses, you document all costs on a shared platform. "I've updated the expense tracker with the latest school fees," you inform your co-parent. This transparency reduces the chance of disputes and ensures both parties are accountable. If a conflict arises, you refer to your conflict resolution protocol. "Let's take a break and discuss this later when we've both had time to think," you suggest. This approach helps maintain a calm and productive conversation, minimizing the emotional impact on your children.

You create a structured and supportive co-parenting environment by establishing clear boundaries and expectations, maintaining a business-like relationship, using parenting apps and tools, and planning for conflict resolution. These strategies help protect your emotional well-being and ensure your children grow up in a stable and nurturing environment.

10.4 Parallel Parenting

Often, traditional methods of co-parenting are not feasible with a narcissistic parent (this was the case in my own experience). This is when parallel parenting becomes necessary. But what is parallel parenting? Parallel parenting is a co-parenting approach used in high-conflict situations where direct communication between the parents is not possible. Each parent is responsible for making decisions during their parenting time without interference from the other parent. Communication is often limited to essential child-related information only. This approach aims to reduce conflict and create a more stable environment for the children, minimizes the need for direct contact between the parents, and can help reduce conflict. In parallel parenting, the co-parents disengage from each other and have minimal direct contact, focusing instead on maintaining separate, parallel lives with the children. This approach. Parallel parenting can provide a structured and peaceful way for parents to co-parent.

10.5 Communicating Effectively with Your Children

Tailoring your communication to match your child's developmental stage is crucial for helping them understand and process their experiences. For younger children, simplifying explanations can make complex issues more digestible. Instead of delving into the intricacies of narcissistic behaviour, you might say, "Sometimes, people can be unkind and make us feel bad, but it's not our fault." Using metaphors or stories can also be effective. For example, explaining difficult concepts through a story about a character they love can make the information more relatable and less intimidating.

As your children grow, providing more detailed information becomes necessary. Older children and teenagers crave understanding and explanations that respect their growing intellect. You might discuss the behaviours they observe, explaining how manipulation and control work. Using age-appropriate language, you can say, "When someone always tries to make you feel wrong or doubt yourself, they are trying to control how you feel and think. This isn't fair to you." This approach informs and validates their observations and feelings, reinforcing their trust in you.

Creating an environment where children feel safe expressing themselves is equally important. Regular family check-ins can be a great way to keep the lines of communication open. Set aside time each week to sit down together and talk about anything on their minds. One-on-one conversations are also valuable. These moments show your children that you are genuinely interested in their thoughts and feelings. Active listening is key. When your child speaks, give them your full attention. Nod, make eye contact, and respond thoughtfully. Validate their feelings by saying things like, "I understand why you feel that way," or "It's okay to feel upset."

Reassuring your children that it's okay to share their thoughts is crucial. They need to know their feelings are valid and they won't be judged or dismissed. Encourage them to talk about their day, worries, and joys. This open dialogue builds trust and helps them feel secure in expressing their emotions. When they share, listen without interrupting or jumping to solutions. Sometimes, they just need to be heard.

Teaching problem-solving skills can empower your children to address and resolve conflicts independently. Role-playing different scenarios can be a fun and educational way to practice these skills. For example, you can act out a situation where they need to stand up for themselves or resolve a disagreement with a friend. After role-playing, brainstorm solutions together. Ask questions like, "What do you think you could do in this situation?" or "How might you handle this differently next time?" Encourage critical thinking and decision-making by letting them come up with their own solutions and offering guidance as needed.

Providing reassurance and support during difficult times is vital for your child's emotional well-being. Affirm their worth and strengths regularly. Simple statements like, "You are so brave," or "I'm proud of how hard you're trying" can boost their self-esteem. Be physically and emotionally present. Sometimes, just being there, offering a hug, or a comforting word can make all the difference. Consistent and unconditional love is the foundation of your child's resilience. Let them know that no matter what happens, you are there for them, supporting and loving them unconditionally.

Imagine a scenario where your child comes home upset after a conflict with their narcissistic parent. You sit down with them, simplifying the explanation of the behaviour they experienced, perhaps using a story to make it relatable. You actively listen as they share their feelings, validating their emotions and reassuring them that it's okay to feel hurt or confused. You then role-play different ways they might handle similar situations in the future, brainstorming solutions together. Throughout the conversation, you affirm their worth and strengths, reminding them of their resilience and your unconditional love. This approach helps them process their emotions and equips them with the skills and confidence to navigate future challenges.

By keeping communication age-appropriate, encouraging open and honest dialogue, teaching problem-solving skills, and providing reassurance and support, you can help your children feel understood, valued, and empowered. These strategies foster a strong, trusting relationship and equip them with the tools they need to thrive, even in the face of adversity.

Chapter 11: Personal Empowerment and Growth

Picture yourself standing at the edge of a vast field, the horizon stretching with endless possibilities. Each step you take represents a new opportunity to reclaim your life and build something beautiful and fulfilling. This is the essence of personal empowerment and growth—recognizing that your path forward is filled with potential and taking proactive steps to shape your future. Setting personal goals is crucial to this part of this journey, providing direction, motivation, and a sense of accomplishment that fuels your recovery.

11.1 Setting Personal Goals for Recovery

Setting personal goals is not just about ticking off a to-do list; it's about giving your life direction and purpose. When you set goals, you create a roadmap for where you want to go, helping you navigate the challenges and opportunities that lie ahead. Goals provide structure and focus, helping you prioritize your efforts and channel your energy into meaningful pursuits. They also serve as milestones along your recovery journey, allowing you to measure your progress and celebrate your achievements. This sense of accomplishment boosts your motivation and self-confidence, encouraging you to keep moving forward. Importantly, goal setting fosters a proactive approach to healing, empowering you to take control of your recovery and make intentional choices that support your well-being.

Balancing short-term and long-term goals is essential for maintaining momentum and staying focused. Short-term goals provide immediate targets to work towards, offering quick wins that boost your motivation and confidence. For instance, a short-term goal might be, "Read one self-help book this month." This goal is manageable and provides a sense of accomplishment within a short timeframe. On the other hand, long-term goals give you something to aspire to, providing a vision for your future and guiding your overall direction. An example of a long-term goal is "Complete a professional certification within the next year." This goal requires sustained effort and commitment but offers significant rewards for personal and professional growth. Creating a vision board can be a helpful tool for visualizing your long-term goals, keeping them top of mind, and inspiring you to stay focused and motivated.

One effective way to set goals is by using the SMART framework. SMART goals are Specific, Measurable, Achievable, Relevant, and Time-bound. This approach ensures that your goals are clear, realistic, and trackable, making it easier to stay committed and see tangible progress.

Interactive Element: Goal-Setting Worksheet

Use the following worksheet to set your SMART goals:

- **Specific**: What exactly do you want to achieve?

- **Measurable**: How will you track your progress?

- **Achievable**: Is this goal realistic, given your current resources and constraints?

- **Relevant**: How does this goal align with your overall purpose and recovery?

- **Time-bound:** What is your deadline for achieving this goal?

Example:

- **Specific**: Exercise for 30 minutes.

- **Measurable**: Three times a week.

- **Achievable**: Yes, within my physical capabilities.

- **Relevant**: Supports my physical and mental health.

- **Time-bound**: For the next month.

Tracking your progress and adjusting your goals as needed is crucial for staying on track and maintaining your commitment. Keeping a goal journal or planner can help you monitor your progress, reflect on your achievements, and identify any obstacles or challenges you encounter along the way. Setting regular check-ins with yourself allows you to assess your progress, celebrate your successes, and make any necessary adjustments to your goals or strategies. Being flexible and open to change is important, as well as recognizing that your goals may evolve as you gain new insights or circumstances change. Adapting your goals based on your experiences and growth ensures they remain relevant and achievable, supporting your ongoing recovery and empowerment.

11.2 Embracing Self-Compassion

Imagine looking at yourself in the mirror and offering the same kindness and understanding you would give to a dear friend. This is the essence of self-compassion, a concept that can be transformative in your healing process. Self-compassion involves three main components: self-kindness, common humanity, and mindfulness. It means treating yourself with the same care and support you would offer someone you love, recognizing that suffering and mistakes are part of the shared human experience, and being mindful of your feelings without becoming overwhelmed by them. Unlike self-pity, which can trap you in a cycle of negativity or self-indulgence, which may lead to unproductive behaviours, self-compassion encourages a balanced and healthy approach to your emotions. Practicing self-compassion can reduce anxiety and depression, lower levels of stress, and improve overall well-being. It helps you build resilience, allowing you to bounce back from setbacks with greater ease and confidence.

One of the practical ways to start embracing self-compassion is through self-compassionate self-talk. This involves replacing self-critical thoughts with language that is kind and supportive. For instance, when you catch yourself thinking, "I can't believe I messed up again," try reframing it to, "It's okay to make mistakes; I am learning and growing." Using affirmations that emphasize kindness and understanding can make a significant difference in how you perceive yourself and your experiences. Another approach is to reframe negative thoughts to be more supportive. Instead of saying, "I'm not good enough," try, "I am doing my best, and that is enough." These simple shifts in language can help you develop a more compassionate and understanding relationship with yourself.

Engaging in specific self-compassion exercises can further help you develop a self-compassionate mindset. One powerful exercise is writing a letter to yourself from the perspective of a compassionate friend. In this letter, offer yourself the same warmth, empathy, and encouragement a close friend would provide. This exercise can help you internalize a more supportive and understanding voice. Another exercise is practicing guided self-compassion meditations, which can help you cultivate feelings of compassion and kindness towards yourself. These meditations often involve visualizing a compassionate figure or repeating phrases that foster self-compassion. Additionally, engaging in self-soothing activities, such as taking a warm bath, reading a favourite book, or spending time in nature, can provide comfort and help you reconnect with a sense of peace and well-being.

Real-life examples of self-compassion can illustrate its transformative power. Consider the story of Sarah, who struggled with intense self-criticism after leaving a toxic relationship. By practicing daily affirmations, she gradually replaced her negative self-talk with supportive and encouraging language. Over time, Sarah significantly improved her self-esteem and overall emotional well-being. Another example is David, who faced numerous setbacks in his healing process. Instead of berating himself for not progressing quickly enough, David used self-compassion to navigate these challenges. He reminded himself that healing is not linear and that it's okay to have difficult days. This mindset allowed him to approach his recovery with patience and kindness, ultimately fostering a more sustainable and positive healing journey.

11.3 Exploring New Hobbies and Interests

Imagine waking up each day with excitement and curiosity, eager to engage in activities that bring you joy and fulfillment. Exploring new hobbies and interests can be a powerful way to support your personal growth and recovery. Engaging in hobbies provides a sense of accomplishment and purpose, giving you something positive to focus on. Whether learning to paint, gardening, or picking up a musical instrument, these activities can reduce stress and promote relaxation, offering a much-needed escape from daily pressures. Hobbies also enhance creativity and problem-solving skills, allowing you to approach challenges with a fresh perspective. Additionally, they help build new social connections and support networks, introducing you to like-minded individuals who share your passions.

Discovering new hobbies requires a bit of self-reflection and exploration. Start by reflecting on past interests and activities that brought you joy. Think about what you loved to do as a child or what you've always wanted to try but never had the time for. Trying out different hobbies through classes or workshops can also be a great way to find what resonates with you. Many community centers, local colleges, and online platforms offer courses in a wide range of subjects, from cooking and photography to woodworking and dance. Seeking inspiration from books, online resources, or friends can also spark new interests. Sometimes, a casual conversation or a social media post can lead you to discover a hobby you hadn't considered before.

However, exploring new hobbies can come with its own set of challenges. One common obstacle is managing time and finding opportunities to engage in hobbies, especially when life feels overwhelming. It can be helpful to think of time in weeks rather than days, allowing you to identify hidden pockets of free time. Be mindful of autopilot activities like checking social media, and consider using that time for hobbies instead. Another barrier is the fear of failure or judgment. It's natural to worry about not being good at something new. However, remember that the goal is to enjoy the process, not achieve perfection. Start small and gradually build confidence by practicing in a supportive environment. Whether it's a beginner's class or a private space at home, create an environment where you feel comfortable exploring and learning.

Real-life examples can illustrate the transformative power of new hobbies. Take the story of Maria, a survivor who discovered a passion for painting. She joined a local art group and found immense joy and fulfillment in expressing herself through colours and canvases. The supportive community she found within the group provided her with both encouragement and new friendships. Another example is Daniel, who took up gardening as a way to connect with nature and find peace. Tending to his plants became meditative, helping him cultivate patience and mindfulness. The simple act of nurturing life brought him a deep sense of satisfaction and serenity, contributing significantly to his emotional well-being.

11.4 Celebrating Small Wins

Imagine the feeling of crossing off a task from your to-do list or hitting a milestone you've been working towards. Celebrating small wins is essential in your recovery process. Recognizing and celebrating these achievements boosts motivation and self-confidence, reinforcing the positive behaviours and habits that support your growth. Each small success provides a sense of accomplishment and progress, reminding you that you are moving forward, even if the steps seem tiny. This practice helps maintain a positive outlook and builds resilience, making tackling larger goals and challenges easier.

To begin recognizing and appreciating your small successes, consider keeping an achievement journal. Dedicate a few minutes each day or week to jot down your accomplishments, no matter how minor they may seem. This could be anything from completing a task you've been putting off to practicing self-care. Sharing your achievements with supportive friends or family members can also amplify the joy and reinforce your progress. Reflecting on your progress during regular self-check-ins helps you stay aware of how far you've come and what you've achieved. These practices highlight your successes and keep you engaged and committed to your recovery journey.

Finding creative ways to celebrate small wins can make the process more enjoyable and meaningful. Treat yourself to a favourite activity or indulgence, like a special meal, a day out, or a relaxing bath. Creating a visual representation of your achievements, such as a success jar or a wall of sticky notes, can serve as a constant reminder of your progress. Each time you achieve a goal, add a note or token to your jar or wall. Planning small rewards for reaching milestones can also be motivating. For example, promise yourself a weekend getaway after completing a major project or achieving a significant goal. These celebrations act as positive reinforcement, encouraging you to keep pushing forward.

Consider the story of Tom, who decided to reward himself with a weekend getaway after reaching a significant goal in his recovery. He had been working tirelessly to rebuild his self-esteem and confidence, and this reward was a way to acknowledge his hard work and dedication. The trip not only provided him with a much-needed break but also served as a powerful reminder of his progress. Another example is Lisa, who celebrated her small wins by organizing a small gathering with friends. Each time she reached a milestone, she invited her closest friends over for a casual get-together. These celebrations helped her stay connected with her support network and reinforced her sense of accomplishment.

Visual aids can be incredibly effective in maintaining motivation and tracking progress. Consider creating a "success jar." Each time you achieve something, no matter how small, write it down on a piece of paper and drop it into the jar. Over time, the jar will fill up with your accomplishments, providing a tangible representation of your progress. On days when you're feeling discouraged, you can pull out a few notes to remind yourself of how much you've achieved. This simple yet powerful tool can help you stay focused and motivated, even when the going gets tough.

In celebrating small wins, you're acknowledging your progress and building a foundation of positive reinforcement that will support your long-term recovery. These celebrations act as milestones, marking your journey and providing motivation to keep moving forward. They remind you that every step, no matter how small, is a step towards healing and empowerment. As you continue to recognize and celebrate your achievements, you'll find that your confidence grows, your resilience strengthens, and your outlook becomes more positive. This practice of celebrating small wins is a crucial part of your recovery, helping you stay engaged, motivated, and hopeful for the future.

As we move forward, we'll explore the importance of maintaining long-term recovery and the strategies to sustain your progress. This next chapter will delve into the practical steps and mindset shifts needed to build a resilient foundation for lasting change.

Chapter 12: Long-Term Recovery and Maintenance

Imagine you're finally stepping out of the storm. The clouds have parted, and rays of sunlight are beginning to warm your face. You've survived the chaos of narcissistic abuse, and now, you're ready to embrace a future filled with hope and possibilities. Yet, this new chapter in your life requires careful navigation to ensure you don't fall back into old patterns. Long-term recovery isn't just about moving on; it's about thriving and building a life where you are in control, confident, and truly happy.

12.1 Preventing Relapse into Abusive Relationships

Recognizing early warning signs is crucial in avoiding a relapse into abusive relationships. Abusers often hide or mask early warning signs, appearing as perfect partners initially. Remember, they will begin with love bombing early on to lower your defences and create a false sense of closeness. It's essential to be vigilant and discerning. Overly controlling behaviour can manifest subtly at first, such as insisting on knowing your whereabouts or dictating your choices. This behaviour might seem like a genuine concern, but it's a red flag. Isolation tactics are another early sign. Abusers may gradually isolate you from friends and family by constantly texting, calling, or planting seeds of doubt about loved ones. If a new partner discourages you from spending time with your support network, take it as a serious warning. The quick progression of the relationship is also a red flag. If someone pushes for rapid commitment, it might seem romantic, but it's often a tactic to entrap you before you can see their true colours.

Establishing non-negotiable boundaries is imperative for protecting yourself from future abuse. Start by defining your personal limits and deal-breakers. What behaviours are you unwilling to tolerate? Write them down and be specific. Communicate these boundaries early in the relationship. It might feel uncomfortable, but it sets the tone for mutual respect. For instance, you might say, "I value my personal space and need time alone to recharge." Enforcing consequences for boundary violations is equally important. If your new partner crosses a line, address it immediately and clearly. For example, "When you dismiss my feelings, it hurts me. If it happens again, I'll need to reconsider our relationship." This approach ensures that your boundaries are respected and you maintain control over your well-being.

Developing a strong support network is another key element in preventing relapse. Having trusted friends and family involved in your relationship decisions can provide much-needed perspective and guidance. They can help you see things you might overlook and offer support when needed. Join support groups for survivors of abuse. These groups provide a sense of community and understanding that can be incredibly validating.

Empower yourself with self-awareness and self-trust. Trusting your instincts is one of the most powerful tools you have. Practicing mindfulness helps you stay present and connected to your inner feelings. Take time each day to sit quietly and observe your thoughts and emotions without judgment. Journaling experiences and reflections on relationship dynamics can also be incredibly insightful. Write about your interactions, noting any behaviours that made you uncomfortable or happy. This practice helps you identify patterns and reinforces your self-awareness. Finally, take time to evaluate your feelings before making decisions. Don't rush into commitments or ignore your gut instincts. If something feels off, give yourself the space to explore why.

Interactive Element: Boundaries Reflection Exercise

Reflect on and write down responses to the following:

- What behaviours are you unwilling to tolerate in a relationship?

- How will you communicate these boundaries early on?

- What consequences will you enforce if your boundaries are crossed?

- Who are the trusted individuals in your life who can help you navigate relationship decisions?

As you move forward, remember that the journey to long-term recovery is ongoing. Each step you take towards recognizing early warning signs, establishing firm boundaries, developing a support network, and trusting yourself brings you closer to a life of empowerment and happiness. Embrace this new chapter with confidence, knowing that you have the tools and strength to build a future where you are truly in control.

12.2 Sustaining Self-Care Practices

Integrating self-care into your daily routine is like planting seeds in a garden. Each small act of self-care nurtures your well-being and helps you grow stronger. One of the first steps is setting aside dedicated time for self-care activities. This might seem challenging initially, especially if you have a busy schedule, but even small time blocks can make a big difference. For instance, you could start by dedicating ten minutes in the morning for a quiet cup of tea or a short meditation session. Creating a self-care schedule or checklist can also be helpful. Write down your planned activities and check them off as you complete them. This keeps you accountable and gives you a sense of accomplishment.

Exploring diverse self-care activities ensures that you cater to all aspects of your well-being. Physical self-care includes activities like exercise, yoga, or dance. Exercise doesn't have to be strenuous; even a gentle walk in the park can uplift your mood and boost your energy levels. Yoga combines physical postures with breath control and meditation, offering both physical and emotional benefits. Dance can be a joyful and liberating way to express yourself, whether in a class or in your living room. Emotional self-care might involve:

- Journaling your thoughts and feelings.

- Engaging in therapy.

- Exploring creative outlets like painting or music.

These activities allow you to process emotions and express yourself freely. Social self-care is equally important. Spend time with loved ones, join clubs or groups that interest you, or participate in community events. These interactions can provide a sense of belonging and support.

Monitoring and adjusting your self-care practices is crucial as your needs and circumstances change. Reflect regularly on what practices are most effective for you. For example, you might find that morning walks are more beneficial than evening ones or that a particular hobby no longer brings you joy. Be open to trying new activities and assessing their impact on your well-being. If you discover a new passion, such as gardening or pottery, incorporate it into your routine. Seeking feedback from trusted individuals can also provide valuable insights. Friends, family, or a therapist might offer suggestions you hadn't considered or notice improvements you might overlook.

Common obstacles to self-care can often feel like insurmountable barriers, but they can be addressed with practical solutions. Time constraints are a frequent challenge. Finding small pockets of time throughout your day can help. Perhaps you can squeeze in a few minutes of deep breathing exercises during your lunch break or listen to a relaxing podcast during your commute. Guilt or feeling undeserving of self-care is another common hurdle. Practicing self-compassion is essential here. Remind yourself that taking care of your well-being is not selfish but necessary. You deserve to feel good and be healthy. Lack of resources can also be a concern. However, there are many affordable or free self-care options available. Community centers often offer low-cost classes, and many online platforms provide free yoga or meditation sessions. Libraries can be an excellent resource for books on self-care, and local parks provide a space for physical activities.

Interactive Element: Self-Care Reflection Exercise

Reflect on your current self-care routine. Write down the activities you engage in and how they make you feel. Identify any gaps or areas where you could introduce new practices. Consider the following questions:

- What self-care activities bring you the most joy and relaxation?

- Are there any new activities you've been wanting to try?

- How can you adjust your routine to better meet your current needs?

- Who in your life can provide support and feedback on your self-care practices?

Incorporating self-care into your daily life is a continuous process. It's about finding what works for you, making adjustments as needed, and maintaining a balance that supports your overall well-being. By integrating these practices, exploring diverse activities, and addressing common obstacles, you can sustain a self-care routine that nurtures your mind, body, and spirit.

12.3 Ongoing Personal Development

Imagine waking up each day with a sense of curiosity and excitement, knowing that each moment holds the potential for growth and discovery. Committing to lifelong learning is about embracing this mindset and continually seeking opportunities to expand your knowledge and skills. Setting personal and professional development goals can provide direction and purpose. Maybe you've always wanted to learn a new language, improve your cooking skills, or advance your career. Taking courses or workshops can be a great way to gain new skills and meet like-minded individuals. Reading books and articles on self-improvement can offer fresh perspectives and practical advice. Each new piece of knowledge is a building block, helping you construct a fulfilling and empowered life.

Engaging in reflective practices is another cornerstone of ongoing personal development. Keeping a reflective journal allows you to document your thoughts, feelings, and experiences, providing valuable insights into your growth. This practice helps you understand patterns in your behaviour and thought processes, making it easier to identify areas for improvement. Scheduling regular self-assessment sessions can help you stay on track with your goals and make necessary adjustments. During these sessions, evaluate your progress and celebrate your achievements. Seeking feedback from mentors or coaches can offer a fresh perspective and guidance. They can help you see blind spots and provide actionable advice to help you grow.

Cultivating new hobbies and interests can add richness and variety to your life. Taking up new hobbies or revisiting old ones can reignite passions and bring joy. Whether it's gardening, painting, or playing a musical instrument, engaging in activities you love can be incredibly fulfilling. Joining clubs, groups, or classes can also be a great way to learn new skills and meet new people. Volunteering or engaging in community service can provide a sense of purpose and connection. It allows you to contribute to something larger than yourself, fostering a sense of belonging and positively impacting your community.

Committing to lifelong learning, engaging in reflective practices, cultivating new hobbies, and setting meaningful goals are integral to ongoing personal development. Each step brings you closer to a more enriched and empowered life.

12.4 Building a Future Beyond Abuse

Creating a vision for your future is like planting a garden. You start with a blank canvas, rich with the potential to grow whatever you desire. Visualization exercises can help you imagine this desired future. Close your eyes and picture yourself in a place where you feel safe and happy. What does it look like? What are you doing? Who is with you? Let these images fill your mind and give you a sense of direction. Creating vision boards can also be a powerful tool. Gather words, symbols, and images that represent your goals and aspirations. Arrange them on a board where you can see them daily. This visual reminder keeps you focused and motivated. Writing a personal mission statement is another way to solidify your vision. Reflect on your values, passions, and long-term goals. Write a concise statement describing what you want to achieve and how you plan to get there. This becomes your guiding star, helping you navigate challenges and stay aligned with your true self.

Establishing a supportive environment is crucial for your growth and well-being. Surround yourself with individuals who uplift you, respect your boundaries, and encourage your growth. These relationships provide a foundation of strength and stability. Creating a safe and nurturing living space is equally important. Your home should be a sanctuary where you feel secure and at peace. Decorate it with items that bring you joy and comfort. Keep it organized and clean, as a clutter-free space can significantly impact your mental state. Engaging in communities that align with your values can also offer a sense of belonging and purpose. Being part of a group with shared interests and values can be incredibly fulfilling, whether it's a local club, volunteer group, or online community.

Developing resilience and adaptability equips you to handle life's inevitable ups and downs. Learning to embrace change and uncertainty is also vital. Life is unpredictable, and being adaptable helps you navigate challenges with grace. Instead of resisting change, view it as an opportunity for growth. Building problem-solving and coping skills further enhances your resilience. When faced with a challenge, break it down into smaller, manageable steps. Think creatively about possible solutions and be willing to try different approaches. These skills help you overcome obstacles and build confidence in your ability to handle whatever comes your way.

Celebrating personal victories and progress is an essential part of your long-term recovery. Reflecting on how far you've come since the abuse can be incredibly empowering. Take time to acknowledge the challenges you've overcome and the growth you've achieved. Share your successes with trusted friends and family. Their support and encouragement can amplify your sense of accomplishment. Rewarding yourself for reaching significant milestones is also important. Whether it's a small treat or a special outing, these rewards reinforce your progress and motivate you to keep moving forward.

You can build a fulfilling and empowered life beyond abuse by creating a vision for your future, establishing a supportive environment, developing resilience, and celebrating your victories. Each step you take brings you closer to a brighter, more hopeful future.

Conclusion

As we come to the end of this journey together, let's take a moment to reflect on the ground we've covered. We began by understanding what narcissistic abuse is and how it manifests. We explored the traits and behaviours of narcissists, the devastating impacts on victims, and how the cycle of abuse traps so many. You've learned not just to recognize these patterns but also how to break free from them.

Throughout the book, we examined immediate relief strategies, like the No Contact rule and the Grey Rock method. These tools help you regain control and start the healing process. We also discussed the importance of rebuilding self-esteem and setting clear boundaries to protect your well-being. From navigating new relationships to understanding legal and safety considerations, each chapter provided practical steps and insights to support your recovery.

The role of therapy and professional help was highlighted as a cornerstone of healing. We delved into mindfulness, holistic healing, and the value of self-care. Parenting and protecting your children were addressed with strategies to build resilience and emotional stability. Finally, we focused on personal empowerment, growth, and long-term recovery, emphasizing the ongoing healing journey.

The key takeaways from our time together are crucial. Recognize the traits of narcissists and understand the cycle of abuse. Implement the No Contact rule when possible, and practice self-validation to reclaim your sense of self. Set and maintain clear boundaries to safeguard your emotional health. Rebuild your self-esteem through affirmations and self-compassion. Seek professional help to navigate the complexities of trauma. These strategies form the backbone of your recovery and empowerment.

Remember, you have the strength and resilience to rebuild your life. You've already taken significant steps by engaging with this book. Recovery is a journey, and every step forward, no matter how small, is a victory. You have the power to create a life filled with peace, joy, and fulfillment.

Now, it's time to put these strategies into action. Continue practicing self-care daily. Seek professional help if you feel overwhelmed. Build a supportive network of friends, family, and fellow survivors. Set new goals and strive for personal growth. Your future is filled with possibilities, and you have the tools to navigate it with confidence.

Don't forget the resources available to you. Utilize online tools, read recommended books, join support groups, and explore therapy options. These resources can provide additional support and insights as you continue your recovery journey.

You are not alone. Healing is possible, and you have already made tremendous progress. Celebrate your achievements, no matter how small, and keep moving forward with hope and determination. You deserve a life free from abuse, filled with love, respect, and happiness.

As I conclude this book, I want to express my deepest gratitude to you for allowing me to share my journey and insights. Writing this book has also been a healing process for me, and I am honoured to be part of your recovery journey.

Thank you for your courage, resilience, and trust. Keep believing in yourself and the beautiful future ahead. You've got this, and I'm here cheering you on every step of the way.

With all my best wishes,

K.C. Lockwood

Keeping the Healing Alive

Now that you have everything you need to heal from narcissistic abuse, it's time to pass on your newfound knowledge and show other readers where they can find the same help.

By simply leaving your honest opinion of this book on Amazon, you'll help guide fellow survivors to the information they're seeking and spread the message of empowerment and recovery. Just scan the QR code below to leave your review.

Thank you for your help. Sharing our experiences keeps the journey to healing alive, and you're helping me to do just that.

Thank you from the bottom of my heart!
K.C. Lockwood

References

- *Narcissistic Personality Disorder in Clinical ...* https://www.ncbi.nlm.nih.gov/pmc/articles/PMC5819598/

- *Narcissistic personality disorder - Symptoms and causes* https://www.mayoclinic.org/diseases-conditions/narcissistic-personality-disorder/symptoms-causes/syc-20366662

- *5 Types of Narcissism and How to Spot Each* https://psychcentral.com/health/types-of-narcissism

- *How Healthy Self-Esteem and Clinical Narcissism Differ* https://www.psychologytoday.com/us/blog/beyond-cultural-competence/202206/how-healthy-self-esteem-and-clinical-narcissism-differ

- *Emotional Exhaustion: What It Is and How to Treat It* https://www.healthline.com/health/emotional-exhaustion

- *Long-Term Effects of Narcissistic Abuse* https://www.charliehealth.com/post/the-long-term-effects-of-narcissistic-abuse

- *Long-Term Effects of Narcissistic Abuse - Charlie Health* https://www.charliehealth.com/post/the-long-term-effects-of-narcissistic-abuse#:~:text=Low%20self%2Desteem%26text=The%20constant%20barrage%20of%20narcissistic,says%2C%20feeling%20worthless%20and%20flawed.

- *How to Break a Trauma Bond: 13 Steps From a Therapist* https://www.choosingtherapy.com/how-to-break-a-trauma-bond/

- *Going No Contact With a Narcissist: Everything You Need ...* https://www.choosingtherapy.com/no-contact-with-a-narcissist/

- *The Grey Rock Method: A Technique for Handling Toxic ...* https://psychcentral.com/health/grey-rock-method

- *Self Validation: DBT Skills, Worksheets, Videos, Exercises* https://dialecticalbehaviortherapy.com/emotion-regulation/self-validation/

- *Self-Care and Recovery After Trauma - Mental Health* https://www.webmd.com/mental-health/ss/slideshow-emotional-trauma-self-care

- *Self-affirmation activates brain systems associated with ...* https://www.ncbi.nlm.nih.gov/pmc/articles/PMC4814782/

- *64 Journaling Prompts for Self-Discovery* https://psychcentral.com/blog/ready-set-journal-64-journaling-prompts-for-self-discovery

- *How to Build Inner Strength & Resilience* https://www.aetna.com/health-guide/how-to-build-resilience.html

- *Overcoming Guilt and Shame After Narcissistic Abuse* https://connectionscounselingutah.com/overcoming-guilt-and-shame-after-narcissistic-abuse-a-journey-to-self-forgiveness

- *Setting Healthy Boundaries in Relationships* https://www.helpguide.org/relationships/social-connection/setting-healthy-boundaries-in-relationships

- *How to Set Boundaries — Examples and Scripts* https://momentumpsychology.com/how-to-set-boundaries-examples-and-scripts/

- *How to Deal with Repeat Boundary Violations* https://betterboundariesworkbook.com/repeat-boundary-violations/

- *Co-Parenting with a Narcissist: Tips for Making It Work* https://www.healthline.com/health/parenting/co-parenting-with-a-narcissist

- *How To Spot Relationship Red Flags* https://health.clevelandclinic.org/domestic-abuse-how-to-spot-relationship-red-flags

- *Healthy Communication Tips - Relationships* https://www.verywellmind.com/managing-conflict-in-relationships-communication-tips-3144967

- *Stages of Healing After Narcissistic Abuse: Rebuilding Trust …* https://salltsisters.com/stages-of-healing-after-narcissistic-abuse-rebuilding-trust/

- *Navigating the Balance between Vulnerability and Self- …* https://www.tajucoaching.com/blog/finding-sweet-spot-navigating-balance-between-vulnerability-and-self-protection

- *What are my rights?* https://refuge.org.uk/what-is-domestic-abuse/my-rights/

- *4 Types of Protective Orders - Hester Law Group* https://www.hesterlawgroup.com/blog/2023/february/4-types-of-protective-orders/

- *Creating a Safety Plan* https://www.kansaslegalservices.org/node/2643/creating-safety-plan

- *Preparing For Custody Mediation With A Narcissist* - https://www.micklinlawgroup.com/preparing-for-custody-mediation-with-a-narcissist/

- *How to go about finding a therapist with experience in ...* https://www.quora.com/How-do-I-go-about-finding-a-therapist-with-experience-in-narcissistic-abuse-recovery

- *What Is The Best Therapy for Narcissistic Abuse?* https://www.charliehealth.com/post/what-is-the-best-therapy-for-narcissistic-abuse

- *Support Groups - DOVE | NewYork-Presbyterian/Columbia ...* https://www.nyp.org/social-work/domestic-and-other-violence-emergencies/dove-support-groups

- *9 Tips, Tools, and Strategies for Narcissistic Abuse Recovery* https://www.healthline.com/health/mental-health/9-tips-for-narcissistic-abuse-recovery

- *Trauma-Informed Mindfulness: A Guide* https://psychcentral.com/health/trauma-informed-mindfulness

- *Meditation-based Approaches in the Treatment of PTSD* https://www.ptsd.va.gov/publications/rq_docs/V28N2.pdf

- *What is somatic therapy?* https://www.health.harvard.edu/blog/what-is-somatic-therapy-202307072951

- *Trauma-Informed Yoga: How it Heals, Benefits, and Poses ...* https://psychcentral.com/health/what-is-trauma-informed-yoga

- *How Narcissistic Parents Affect Mental Health in Children* https://modernchangenc.com/how-narcissistic-parents-affect-mental-health-in-children/

- *How Narcissistic Parenting Can Affect Children* https://www.psychologytoday.com/us/blog/the-legacy-of-distorted-love/201802/how-narcissistic-parenting-can-affect-children

- *Helping Children Cope With a Narcissistic Parent* https://www.psychologytoday.com/ca/blog/living-on-automatic/202301/helping-children-cope-with-a-narcissistic-parent

- *Co-Parenting With a Narcissist: Tips and Strategies* https://www.custodyxchange.com/topics/custody/special-circumstances/co-parenting-with-narcissist.php

- *How to Set Realistic and Achievable Goals for Recovery* https://www.pinelandsrecovery.com/how-to-set-realistic-and-achievable-goals-for-recovery/

- *11 SMART Goals Examples For Life Improvement* https://www.lifehack.org/864427/examples-of-personal-smart-goals

- *Cultivating Self-Compassion in Trauma Survivors* https://self-compassion.org/wp-content/uploads/2015/08/Germer.Neff_.Trauma.pdf

- *How Hobbies Improve Mental Health - USU Extension* https://extension.usu.edu/mentalhealth/articles/how-hobbies-improve-mental-health

- *Early Warning Signs of Abuse* https://www.nomore.org/early-warning-signs-of-abuse/

- *Setting Healthy Boundaries in Relationships* https://www.helpguide.org/relationships/social-connection/setting-healthy-boundaries-in-relationships

- *Self-Care and Recovery After Trauma - Mental Health* https://www.webmd.com/mental-health/ss/slideshow-emotional-trauma-self-care

- *Thriving After Narcissistic Abuse: Rebuilding a Life of Empowerment and Happiness* https://www.goodtherapy.org/blog/thriving-after-narcissistic-abuse-rebuilding-a-life-of-empowerment-and-happiness/

Made in the USA
Middletown, DE
18 October 2024

62872176R00088